NIGELLA LAWSON

A BIOGRAPHY

NIGELLA LAWSON
A BIOGRAPHY

Gilly Smith

Fort Lee, New Jersey

Published by Barricade Books Inc.
185 Bridge Plaza North
Suite 308-A
Fort Lee, NJ 07024

www.barricadebooks.com

Published by arrangement with Andre Deutsch Limited, London,
England.

A copy of this title's Cataloging-in-Publication Data is available
upon request from the Library of Congress.

ISBN 1-56980-299-8

First Printing
Printed in Canada

Contents

The publishers would like to thank the following sources for their kind permission to reproduce the pictures in this book.

Insert 1

Picture 1: Getty Images/Hulton Archive; Picture 2: Dafydd Jones; Picture 3: Dafydd Jones; Picture 4: Topham Picture Point/Topfoto.co.uk; Picture 5: Topham Picture Point/Topfoto .co.uk; Picture 6: Empics/PA; Picture 7: Dafydd Jones; Picture 8: Empics/Pa

Insert 2

Picture 1: Topham Picture Point/Uppa/Topfoto.co.uk; Picture 2: Rex Features/Richard Young; Picture 3: Rex Features/Nils Jorgensen; Picture 4: Topham Picture Point/Topfoto.co.uk; Picture 5: Getty Images/Dave Bennett; Picture 6: Getty Images/Dave Bennett; Picture 7: Getty Images/Gustavo Caballero; Picture 8: Rex Features

Every effort has been made to acknowledge correctly and contact the source and/or copyright holder of each picture and Andre Deutsch Limited apologizes for any unintentional errors or omissions that will be corrected in future editions of this book.

Introduction

1999, Shepherd's Bush, West London

Nigella Lawson, journalist, author and mother of two young children, is in her kitchen in a rather unassuming basement on Goldhawk Road. She's putting her make-up on; nothing too fussy – a bit of mascara and some lipstick. She digs into the Whistles bag next to her and picks out a couple of little tops, holding them up to the light, and calls to the dark-haired young woman unpacking a bag of food by the larder to ask her which she thinks she should wear. Hettie Potter, a home economist in her late twenties, puts down the tin of tomatoes and suggests the one with short sleeves. 'Can't show my arms,' replies Nigella, settling for the long-sleeved version.

They look over to the crew of men bustling around her kitchen for approval – and get none. They're busy taping cable to her floor, angling light boxes and installing huge film lights to turn this dark family kitchen into a surreally bright television studio. And besides, they don't care if her arms look fat.

Director Bruce Goodison, sexily scruffy in his mid-thirties, circles Nigella, holding a small camera. He's charming her,

1

teasing her with his endless questions about what she's going to be cooking, why she doesn't wear a brighter red lipstick, how she's going to feel when she's a TV superstar. She barely notices the camera as she tells him her running order for the show, blots her lips and pops one of the cookies she and Hettie baked yesterday afternoon into his mouth.

John Diamond, journalist and broadcaster, husband of Nigella, father of two small children and associate producer on the show, walks in and scribbles a note for Bruce. He reads it and laughs before throwing it in the bin. They smile conspiratorially. Bruce asks Hettie to quickly whip up some cream.

The lights are set. Sound recordist Chris Syner is fixing a microphone into Nigella's hair (a bra is no place for a microphone with *this* woman), and cameraman Neville Kidd is waiting for the director's command. Finally it's time. Nigella moves over to the worktop as Hettie moves into the background.

'Stand by, everybody,' shouts Bruce. 'Roll tape. And ... action.'

CHAPTER ONE

A disagreeable state

Nigella Lawson was born on 6 January 1960, a Capricorn, the first daughter of three and the second child of Vanessa Salmon, socialite, beauty and heiress to the Lyons Corner House dynasty, and Nigel Lawson, future Chancellor of the Exchequer under the UK's first female prime minister, Margaret Thatcher. No wonder she spent her first twenty years alternating between a shy recluse at home and an attention-seeking rebel at school.

Named after a man – and not just any man – she could at least comfort herself with the fact that her name also means 'love-in-a-mist', a wispy member of the buttercup family found in hedgerows whose seeds taste rather lovely when sprinkled on flatbread. And her younger sisters were named Thomasina and Horatia. Apparently this was not inspired by her father's vanity or her parents' disappointment at producing only one *real* boy, but a strange, bohemian affectation of her mother's, who plundered *The Times*'s obituary pages for names in a way that parents look to gossip columns these days. 'I always wanted to be called Caroline,' Nigella told Sally Vincent in the *Guardian*. 'Carolines were always very nice in books.' She used to make up names for herself. 'Mercedes Wainwright was the best one.' But by the time her name was a byline in a series of national newspapers, Nigella Lawson had decided against reducing herself to the initials NL and, if not quite shouting loud and proud, she was finding that rolling the name around her own mouth was no longer quite so distasteful. 'Maybe it put mettle in my spine,' she says. 'It's my name, and I own it.'

Her early years were privileged but melancholy, despite being surrounded by three siblings. She had a difficult relationship with her mother, and there was a frosty relationship between her parents, which left her in a disagreeable state. 'I wasn't suited to dependence and the lack of autonomy, to such an extent it put me off having children for a long time. I thought, "How can I inflict childhood on anyone?" ' In and out of homes in Kensington, Chelsea and Holland Park, she flitted through social circles straight out of the pages of *Harpers and Queens*, and was dragged sullenly through five different schools between the ages of nine and eighteen.

'I was never expelled,' she said. 'I was unruly in class but I didn't deal drugs or go off with boys. I've never been good at authority. Even with my own children at parents' evenings I'm not altogether sure I'll behave correctly.' She admitted that her parents 'may have been asked to take me out. I was just disruptive, good at schoolwork but rude, I suspect, and too highly strung.' When handed her maths paper at 11 Plus, she smiled sarcastically, handed it back and said, 'Sorry, I don't do this.' Needless to say she failed. It may have been the arrogance of youth, or perhaps she learnt it from her elders;

her mother excused her from taking a compulsory subject, telling the headmaster, 'Nigella is too highly strung for geography.'

Although her school reports described Nigella as 'disruptive', at home she was quiet and spent most of her time with her head in a book – preferably something dark like Thomas Mann. 'My parents often thought they'd brought the wrong child home from school,' said Nigella with a laugh on *Desert Island Discs*.

Coming from a family of fierce intellect and exceptionally high expectations, there was never any question that she wouldn't be bright. 'I'm quite serious and was always going to be a novelist,' she said. 'I wrote a book when I was nine and a play which takes the form of two turtles on a train called "Recreation" and "Activity" – frightfully precocious. Thank God I found unpretentious salvation in the kitchen.'

Nigella finally found her academic feet at Godolphin and Latymer, now an independent girls' school in Hammersmith, but a state grammar school at the time; it counts Hattie Jaques, Davina McCall and Una Stubbs among its old girls. She began to excel – just in time for her A Levels. 'They were very pleased with how I did,' she remembers, 'and said it was a pity I hadn't started there sooner.' Which of course she could only have done with an 11 Plus under her belt.

It was here that she met her lifelong friend, Emily Lawson-Tancred. 'She was very successful at school,' said Emily when I asked her about her previous behavior at her boarding schools and her reputation as a disruptive student. 'She wasn't a swot but she did very well. She was always very friendly with everyone'. They became inseparable and would spend every afternoon at each other's homes. 'By the time I met her, they were living in Bedworth Square, just off the Kings Road in Chelsea. I don't know what happened, but they had lost a lot of the family money. When her parents got divorced a few years later, they both bought their own homes in London so there wasn't a lot of money around.'

Like most attention-seeking grumpy teenagers, her relationship with her mother was at the center of it all. 'There were many complicated reasons for it, and it did resolve itself,' she explained. 'My mother was captivating, charming, but with unpredictable mood swings. She was very young when I was born, and perhaps had too much invested in her looks. I learned pretty early on that a good profile can only take you so far, and it's better to have energy. I'm a mixture of too much energy and too much melodramatic whining. I exhaust people.'

Vanessa Salmon was just nineteen when she married Nigel Lawson, then already blazing the trail that many of his family would follow as a smart young journalist. Vanessa had hoped to become a ballerina, but like most other nice girls of the 1950s, she gave it all up to become a mother. Dominic was born in 1957, then Nigella in 1960, Thomasina in 1962 and Horatia four years later.

Vanessa's was also a privileged childhood, surrounded by power and money. One uncle, Cyril Salmon, was a successful judge and Lord of Appeal between 1972 and 1980, and another, Samuel, was mayor of Hammersmith between 1968 and 1969. Her great-grandfather, Barnett Salmon, had founded one of London's most influential catering businesses, The Lyons Corner House empire under J. Lyons and Co., one of the most inventive companies of the time, diversifying into fast food products and outlets, creating the UK ice-cream market with Lyons Maid, and arguably influencing much of the change in our national food consumption. It remained under the control of the Salmon family until it was bought out by Allied Breweries which eventually became Allied Lyons. By the 1980s it was sold off to various different companies, including Nestlé which bought much of its ice cream products.'

The Lyons Corner Houses in Coventry Street, the Strand and Tottenham Court Road, and the Maison Lyons at Marble Arch and Shaftsbury Avenue first appeared in London 1909 and were huge restaurants on four or five levels with a vast number of waiting staff, known as 'nippies' for their speedy service. Each floor had its own restaurant style, with orchestras playing throughout the day and evening, and a Food Hall packed with speciality produce, hams, cakes, pastries, hand-made chocolates, fruit from the Empire and wines, cheeses and flowers which rivalled the more upmarket Harrods and Fortnum & Masons in the pre-war years. Lyons Corner Houses even had hair dressing salons, telephone booths, theatre booking agencies and a food delivery service to any address in London twice a day.

Lyons also opened restaurants across London and the provinces. The Steak House was another of their brands which opened up after the Second World War all around London and its leafy, prosperous suburbs, spreading as far afield as Tunbridge Wells, Brighton, Bristol, Norwich, and Gloucester. It was part of a culinary experience offered to all classes of diner and unknown in Britain, and was to kick-start a less savory one year later as well, as its own demise, when it introduced self service and fast food with the Wimpy chain in the 1950s.

Stuck at boarding school throughout her childhood – even in the holidays whenever her mother decided against having the children at home – Vanessa took the first opportunity to flee the Salmons. Her marriage to Nigel was a meeting of moneyed families. The Lawsons lived in the wealthy North London village of Hampstead, 'complete with nanny, cook and parlourmaid', as Nigel writes in his memoirs, *The View from No.11*. Nigel's father was a successful tea broker in The City, and owned his own small company; the coincidence is not lost on Nigella who refers to both sides of the family as 'pushers' . Nigel's maternal grandfather was also wealthy, the senior partner of a firm of stockbrokers, and he grew up in a large extended family, much of which still lives in the Hampstead area, proper Jews with names like Goldberg and Goldman.

For Nigel, being Jewish was not necessarily a good career move, and it is interesting to note that he failed to mention his Jewishness in his memoirs. He had a suitably *goy* education at Westminster and Oxford, but then married a good Jewish girl, which was very possibly the last thing he did that pleased the *mishporcha* (Yiddish for 'extended family'). There were precious few Jews in either the media or politics at the time. Alan Watkins, a newspaper colleague of Lawson's, said that the cultural mix was very different in the 1960s than today. 'The media were run by Celtic and Commonwealth communities: the Irish, Scottish, Welsh, New Zealanders and Australians. Jews were going into law and other business where there was more money. It was only when the media became more showbiz, and started to offer more opportunities for making more money, that they started to attract more Jewish people.' He said that Nigel Lawson

8

didn't even pay lip service to his culture as he climbed the ranks. 'When he became editor of the *Spectator*, the *Jewish Chronicle* asked him if he would like to send a message to its Jewish readers, and he declined, saying that he had nothing to say whatsoever.'

Rabbi Pini Dunner, who until recently presided over the Saatchi Synagogue in North London, disagreed that Nigel needed to hide his Jewishness for the sake of becoming a Member of Parliament (he was elected for Blaby in Leicestershire in 1974). 'I don't think that it was too difficult for Jews to work their way into British politics in the seventies. Keith Joseph certainly didn't need to hide his Jewishness.' He was quick to add, though, that the ultimate British Jewish politician was Disraeli, who converted to Christianity and made sure all his children followed suit. He maintained a pride in his racial origins, but, Dunner reminded me, 'Conversion is the most rapid way to integrate into British society. Nigel Lawson had two generations of liberal Jews dominating his background. He's like most Jewish people in that he wanted to assimilate. We're like chameleons, always seeking to blend in.'

Vanessa's family had already broken ranks and chosen to live outside the 'ghettos' of East and North London in Ham Common in South West London. Vanessa and Nigel also chose the white, upper-middle-class neighbourhood of Chelsea to raise their brood of four. 'I would never have thought of Vanessa as being Jewish,' said Peregrine Worsthorne, Vanessa's friend, and a former colleague of both Nigel and Dominic. 'She would make foods like liver pâté, the kind of food you read about in Saul Bellow and Philip Roth, but that was about it.' Nigella told journalist Tamasin Day-Lewis that even if Vanessa's roots didn't show much outside the kitchen, inside the legacy was more pervasive. 'Most of my cooking I learned from watching my mother. It was very influenced by Jewish culture, lots of flour-based sauces, which are a very European thing, and roast chicken with leeks in white sauce, very Hungarian. Our family always talked about food. It is part of Jewish culture.'

Nigel, fresh from Oxford, decided early on a political career, and saw that getting inside the real instrument of power, the media, was a clever first step. According to those who worked with him he was 'tremendously clever', and quickly worked his way up to the editorship of the *Spectator*, a magazine with a reputation for political influence. The Lawsons were unusual among Nigel's peers in the media. Alan Watkins worked under Nigel's editorship in the 1960s. 'I remember going round to Nigel's with a couple of colleagues for a working breakfast when I was working on the *Spectator*. We were expecting a couple of slices of toast on the table, nothing more. But we'd never seen anything like it before – there was a feast of Edwardian grandeur on the sideboard, with kidneys and all sorts of wonderful things on offer. We were in our early thirties and you just wouldn't expect that of another journalist of the same age. It was very upper middle class.'

Nigel was extraordinarily aspirant, with his sights set firmly on Parliament. 'Nigella used to talk about the parties in their house,' Emily told me. 'They had all the names of the day there. It wasn't at all like my house.' These days Nigella is blasé about the kind of guests who passed through her parents' doors. She told Andrew Harrison in *Word* magazine that she barely noticed Margaret Thatcher's presence in her life. 'I met her, yes, but I honestly can't remember much about her. I was quite young at the time and I didn't pay all that much attention. We might have given her a lift home or something.' Unlike her brother, Nigella said that she was never interested in her father's scene, although she conceded, 'It was an interesting home. There were a lot of interesting people and a lot of talk, a lot of food, a lot of talk.'

He had already shown his political leanings when he took advantage of a mortgage offer from Kensington Council to buy a huge house in Hyde Park Gate. As an aspiring political animal, he was hauled over the coals by the Labour Government of the time. But, as Alan Watkins said, he had done nothing wrong. 'The local council was offering mortgages at very favourable rates, but as he was a reasonably rich sort of character it wasn't really for people like him. If you offer services, people will take them up.'

In the 1970s a good housewife's job was to cook beautifully and raise the children effortlessly. Cook beautifully she did – although Nigella remembers the resentment her mother felt at having to satisfy her self-imposed high standards – and she also raised children, although with rather more effort than she might have imagined. Peregrine Worsthorne remembers her as an attentive although rather anxious mother. 'She loved her children and talked about them a lot. She was never one of those absentee mothers. I remember going out with her with the children when Nigella and Dominic would have been about eight and ten, and they did look angelic. They were very sweet. But I remember that there was a certain tension around them all when they were together.'

Parents of strong-willed children may well recognize this feeling of walking on eggshells, with their children's unpredictable moods likely to ruin a shopping trip at any moment. But Vanessa, who was 'emotionally strong' according to Worsthorne, was not overbearing. 'She was never rude or domineering, although she may well have been rather controlling. I would imagine that she would have had rather high expectations on how they behaved and how they looked.' Nigella's friend Sarah Johnson says she got the impression that Vanessa was rather unpredictable and volatile, not a trait she passed on to her eldest daughter. 'Nigella doesn't have a temper at all,' she said. 'My mother and I really only got to know each other when I was at university,' Nigella told *Eve* magazine. 'It was always a difficult relationship. I was very shy as a child, and I remember her saying, rather cruelly, "Why are you so shy? Who do you think is interested in you, anyway?"'

Peregrine Worsthorne was very close to Vanessa during her marriage to Nigel, and particularly later when she was more happily married to Sir Freddie Ayer. He says that she found Nigel Lawson 'pompous, greedy and far too interested in politics'. His first memory was of her pointing her husband out at a party and saying, much to Worsthorne's surprise, 'See that man over there? Isn't he awful?'

Nigella calls her mother's moods 'atmosphering'. 'She would never say exactly why she was angry,' she told Sue

Lawley. 'There would be a silent beam around her' that the children found impenetrable. Was this a reflection of the resentments felt by a beautiful woman married to someone she disliked, or the sulks of an energetic socialite chained to the nursery, grabbing control where she could?

The mysteries around Nigella's sullen childhood probably amount to little more than the fact that she was a sensitive child in a home where food and food obsession took the place of intimate chats. It seems that she didn't learn how to be emotionally articulate in the family home. She has described her father as 'emotionally remote'. Certainly the publicity photograph of Nigel much later as Chancellor in the run-up to the 1985 Budget, in which he is playing French cricket in the Leicestershire countryside of his constituency with his new family, shows him as a man out on a limb. 'What disturbed me,' wrote William Deedes in the *Spectator* about the picture, 'was the Chancellor's appearance in a dark three-piece suit, with matching collar and tie.'

Vanessa, bored and beautiful, with an increasingly absent husband, craved approval from other men. Add this to her resentment of the mind-numbing day-to-day needs of young children and the displaced energy of a fine mind, and one can begin to understand why Nigella experienced a 'silent beam' around her mother, and the tone of their tricky relationship. For her mother to take such pleasure in her social life must have given a clear message to her young children about where her priorities lay. 'Most men I knew fell madly in love with Vanessa,' remembers Alan Watkins. 'She was very beautiful and flirtatious. She wasn't my type at all – she was far too small and thin and wispy and pale. I was very much in the minority though. I wouldn't say that I felt very comfortable with her.'

'She was enormously adventurous,' says Peregrine Worsthorne, 'and great company.' He recalls the impetuous moment in Brighton during a Conservative Party conference when they were sitting together in a restaurant discussing how much she admired his shirt. 'Would you like to wear it?' he asked, and before Nigel could do anything to stop it or head off the professional disgrace that both he and Worsthorne would experience, his wife and the editor of the *Sunday Telegraph* swapped shirts, revealing rather more of Vanessa than was respectable for a Tory wife. 'Either she wasn't wearing a bra at all, or it wasn't much of one. She *was* very mischievous,' he giggled.

Her desire to draw attention to herself was also an opportunity to have a snipe at her husband whenever possible, and her occasional flings which overstepped the mark would have been well known to Nigel – and just about everyone else around. 'She was jolly unfaithful to Nigel,' Alan Watkins said. 'She asked a friend of mine to go away to Paris for a weekend with her. She went to the airport and waited for him, and when he didn't turn up she went home again. I don't think she was very happy at all with Nigel.'

Nigel may have been tiresome and useless as far as Vanessa was concerned, but in the workplace he was a determined man according to those who worked with him. Peregrine Worsthorne had a twenty-eight-year tenure at the *Sunday Telegraph* from 1961, and was Deputy Editor for three years during Nigel's period as City Editor, but quit to edit the *Spectator* in 1966. 'I found him very cold; he certainly made sure that he got what he wanted. If he wanted more space on his city page, he'd be ruthless in getting it even if it meant treading on someone else's toes.' Many years later Worsthorne was sacked by the editor of the *Sunday Telegraph*, a certain Dominic Lawson, which was an eerily familiar experience. 'Dominic can be callous in human relations – not at all like the sweet little boy he once was.'

Nigella's memories of her mother, or at least those she shares with the outside world, are a mix of cooking, bad moods, parties and beautiful clothes. She told Sue Lawley that she chose 'Sugar Sugar' by the Archies as her first record to take with her to her fantasy desert island because it brought back memories of her mother shopping at Biba in High Street Kensington for 'maxi dresses with lovely dusty high pink suede boots', adding in a vaguely melancholic way that it 'reminds me of my childhood in a positive way'. Her school-friend, Emily Lawson-Tancred, says that although Vanessa was always beautifully dressed she was always proud of the fact that she could find a bargain. 'She looked as if she had just come out of Bond Street, but if someone commented on her dress, she'd say proudly, "Twenty pounds from C&A." '

Nigella learned early that being beautiful mattered, and that her mother inhabited quite a different world to the one the rest of us live in. 'All babies find their mother's face beautiful. So it's not a question of discovering that my mother was, but of never having that moment of disillusionment on discovering she wasn't.' Being the daughter of a beautiful woman can be difficult. 'The thing about the beautiful is that not only do people want to look at them, they want to be looked at by them; I could sense how desperate everyone was for what one novelist has called in another context "the bene-diction of her gaze".' Beauty can be a trap for those blessed with astonishing looks, though, with women freezing and men drooling in their company. For Nigella, a shy young woman, she found her mother not only enchanting and unlike other mothers, but a perfect act which was almost impossible to follow. 'The terror of the competition means it's safer almost not to be there, to fade into the unnoticeable background,' she observed.

Most women have probably shared the moment when both mother and daughter respond to the wolf whistle and wonder whom it was for. Nigella remembers it as the experience that prompted her to put on weight. 'I don't know how she knew it was at me and not at her, but she said – not entirely jokingly – "That's it. I'm never going out with you again." ' Nigella never experienced a gracious handing over of the crown from mother to daughter. 'I knew so resolutely when I was in my early twenties that I didn't ever want to have a face instead of a life.'

Vanessa was still stunning at forty-eight when she died of liver cancer. Nigella says part of her is trapped in her world. 'She didn't grow old. She was always beautiful.'

Fading into the background is a way of withholding, of having some control over how much of yourself you share. The teenage Nigella chose not to share herself with her mother. 'I was so introverted that my mother thought I was autistic,' Nigella told the journalist Sally Knatchbull. 'I was a quiet teenager, full of angst. In a way that was a blessing. People who have fabulous childhoods have this sense that nothing is ever going to be that good again. I have the feeling that nothing will ever be that bad. I used to be prone to depression, but there's nothing like unhappiness to cure you of depression.' That, or food.

CHAPTER TWO

Comfort food

Comfort food is at the heart of Nigella's culinary philosophy, and it came from her mother's kitchen. She learned early that cooking is about 'what you want to eat; and if you put yourself into what you are cooking, then it will be original', as she wrote in her *Vogue* column many years later. 'That, more than anything, is my mother's culinary legacy. What I remember is how she cooked, what we ate; no specifications, few admonishments.'

Nigella learned to cook as a child, 'not for my benefit but because my mother believed in child labor. Dominic wasn't made to cook at all and generally he doesn't do much. But he can make a good hollandaise, which is rather difficult.' She and her sisters, particularly Thomasina who was only sixteen months younger, grew up in the kitchen, chopping, tasting, blending sauces, and she reckons that hollandaise was possibly the first thing she ever made too. Her younger sister, Horatia, remembers coming in as a teenager late at night and finding her mother making mayonnaise in her nightie at three in the morning. 'She found it very soothing,' she said.

Nigella knew how she felt. Making mayonnaise, she writes in *How to Eat*, was comparable to her experience of reading Henry James as a teenager. 'I read him with uncorrupted pleasure. Then when I was eighteen or so, someone older, cleverer, whose opinions were offered gravely, asked me whether I didn't find James very difficult, as she always did. Until then, I had no idea that I might, and I didn't. From that moment, I couldn't read him but self-consciously; from then on, I did find him difficult.' Similarly, her breezy easy stirring of the weekly batch of mayonnaise became clumsy and intense, and often ended in a curdled mess. 'When confidence is undermined or ruptured,' she writes, 'it can be difficult to do the simplest things, or to take any enjoyment even in trying.'

She realized by the age of fourteen that while she and her Betty Crocker family had been relying on taste and smell, the world had discovered cook books. Mrs Beeton's books were the nearest the young Nigella ever got to a recipe. Her love of the kind of unfussy cooking that has made her famous comes, she says, from a Mel Calman cartoon which was scotch taped to her mother's cooker showing a woman slaving over a hot stove: 'One man's meat is another woman's Sunday gone.'

It wasn't just her mother who had her busy in the kitchen. 'My grandmother and I used to cook together on Fridays. I don't know whether this meant it was a pre-school exercise or whether we spent those days together during vacations, but I remember being deposited at her house in the morning, walking to the local butcher's and buying strange delicacies we'd cook together in her big, airy kitchen with its black-and-white checkerboard floor.'

While most sullen teenagers rebel against their parents, Nigella followed her parents' rules even into her forties. 'My mother always cooked a ham at Christmas, and so do I,' she wrote in *Feast*. On salads: 'My mother was fanatical, and her aesthetic has seeped into my bloodstream; my father takes the same line. Do not even think of adding your tomatoes; keep them separate.' On soaking: 'My mother always soaked anchovies in milk, just as she did kidneys and chicken livers, therefore so do I.'

The menu in the Lawson household was often unheard of in most British kitchens and inspired by the catering dynasty at Lyons House. The taramasalata, spaghetti al olio, lasagne and moussaka that Vanessa Salmon was knocking up may be staples in many families nowadays, but back in the 1960s they were extremely unusual in Britain, even in swinging London. The 'dressing-soused peppers striated with anchovies', moules marinières and eggy lemony sauces Nigella wrote about in her *Vogue* column were straight out of Elizabeth David's seminal books, such as *Mediterranean Food, French Country Cooking, Italian Food* and *French Provincial Cooking* which plucked Britain out of its post-war austerity and filled its kitchens with the smell of garlic.

The British palate was shaped by the limitations of the time, with home-grown meat and vegetables providing the staples of the war and post-war diet. Unlike the people of the Mediterranean, where food was so much more pleasurable, we lived on an island too cold to sun-dry our tomatoes, and where olives would never tumble down hillsides before being carted off to the local mill to become oil. Living off our land was dull but hearty, with heavy meats and big sauces to keep off the chill. This type of eating was entrenched in our national psyche until the 1970s when the devastating combination of European efficiency directives to farmers, which often destroyed habitats and the contours of the countryside, and the introduction of fast food drastically altered our relationship with food.

Colin Spencer, food historian and author of *British Food*, thinks we were not alone among European countries in losing touch with our culinary heritage. 'Factory farming made food cheap, but lacking in quality, nutrition and flavor. Food for the majority declined in all the Western industrialized countries.' Spencer believes that the influence of the Common Market had little to do with it. 'We began to lose our relationship with our land much earlier, in the seventeenth, eighteenth and nineteenth centuries, because of the enclosure acts, and the fact that our industrial revolution began far earlier than any other European country.'

Spencer says that we often do not recognize the depth of our culinary culture, and our history of helping ourselves to foods we fancy. 'People always mention the influence of Elizabeth David from the fifties onwards,' he said. 'But all those Mediterranean influences were brought in by the Anglo-Normans from 1100 on throughout the Middle Ages. We have always loved spicy dishes; ginger early became a firm favorite. We were heavily influenced by the Persian cuisine (sweet and sour, and the use of flowers in cooked dishes) from that time, unlike Paris who eschewed such foreign influences. Our national culture is one that has always borrowed from other cultures and then anglicized the influences. British India from 1700 on brought in ketchups and curries, and just about every cook book must have recipes for them thereafter. Some cultures that came here tended to be insular, like the Jewish one, but that's because of persecution. If the English decided they liked a flavor they took it over and made it their own.'

During the 1960s the Bohemian vanguard of mass tourism were heading off to the far-flung beaches of Spain, France and even India, and a few were already bringing back the exotic flavors they had tasted for their friends to try. 'Yes, package holidays helped to popularize Mediterranean foods and flavors,' said Spencer, 'but these were in our genes from ten generations back. Pizza today is a commonplace, popular food, as it was in the thirteenth, fourteenth and fifteenth centuries, bought from cook shops and eaten in the streets. Nothing is particularly new. This was urban food. You didn't get a ploughman eating it because there weren't rural cook shops.'

Nigella too was travelling in her summers, and says that she was fascinated by the smells and tastes encountered on trips to Norway with a beloved au pair, and France where she had been 'sent off' aged sixteen to stay with some friends of her parents in Paris. 'They did lapin aux pruneaux and blanquette de veau,' she told Tamasin Day-Lewis in *Waitrose* magazine. 'I remember coming back and cooking pigeon for my father. It's helpful having a greedy father.' It doesn't really matter what the flavors are once the boundaries have been pushed; the bruising of the garlic, the grinding of the spices, the long slow cooking of the lamb and the chopping and chatting are what makes a good meal in a family where food has always been much more than a pit stop.

Her childhood was full of eccentric and eclectic forays with food, which turned into unforgettable tastes and smells that have pervaded her cookery writing, food columns and TV shows ever since, bringing chocolate limes, whitebait starters (Nigel's and Thomasina's favourite), ginger jam (her grand-mother's), liptauer ('*the* deli counter delicacy of my childhood') and Camp coffee bouncing back to life at the mention of their names. Her mother's kitchen smelled of lemon and garlic, and she says that every lemon roasted chicken, every tang of slicing lemons still brings her mother's memories flooding back.

Her maternal grandfather ate his strawberries with pepper, which as a child Nigella considered odd. Now, of course, she realizes it's the *only* way. Even Nigella's tastes were unusual; as a child she hated ice cream, although she was more than happy to accompany her great aunt on regular visits to the ice-cream parlor at the Fountain at Fortnum & Masons – if only for the experience.

The Salmons and Lawsons might have been Jews by birth, but these were families which had been here for so long that they were almost aristocracy in Britain. When it came to 25 December, they adopted the best of both tradi-tions. Like most Christmases *en famille*, it was a tense affair. 'My mother would over-work and over-shop and always burst into tears at some point in the proceedings,' Nigella told Harriet Lane in the *Observer*. 'And also because my parents made us open our presents after lunch, so of course all you wanted to do was get through lunch and get to the presents. But I always liked the taste of it.' Her grand-mother liked Christmas lunch so much, she even cooked the whole thing again on Midsummer's Day. 'There are two Christmas traditions I've inherited from my mother,' she told Lane. 'One is the feeling that Christmas isn't complete if you haven't got a ham as well as a turkey. It means that the leftovers are much better. And in a curious way, despite the fact that we're talking about Christmas and ham, it's a very Jewish thing to want to provide a huge spread. I always cook for eight, but make enough for thirty, so this year I thought I might as well have enough people to eat it. The other thing is putting ground almonds in the brandy butter, which makes it slightly marzipan-ish.'

Her mother might have cooked like a dream, but she didn't eat. She certainly didn't eat puddings, nor did she – or her grandmothers – make them, which Nigella says in *How to Eat* left her unconfident in her baking. Her first cake was a mocha layer cake from a Mrs Beeton recipe for her sister Thomasina's ninth birthday when she was eleven – and of course the Salmon-Lawsons did not normally *do* recipes. 'I didn't acquire early in life that lazy confidence, that instinct (in baking). When I cook a stew I have a sense, automatically, of whether I want to use red or white wine, of what will happen if I add anchovies or bacon. But when I bake I feel I lack that instinct.' *How to be a Domestic Goddess* is a homage to her inner pastry chef, claiming the smells and tastes that were never developed at her mother's side.

'I like to think that I made cupcakes as a child,' Nigella told Justine Picardie, whose charity the Lavender Trust sold Nigella's lavender cupcakes in Harvey Nicholls in memory of her sister Ruth, who died of breast cancer in 1997. 'I probably didn't. My mother wasn't someone who baked cakes – she never did puddings, never did sweet things. I started making them with my own children when they were very young, for birthday parties and so on. But I noticed that it was their friends' parents whose faces lit up when they saw the cupcakes. I've got absolutely no wish to be a child again, but perhaps making cupcakes is an idealized version of a childhood I didn't have. Maybe people who had happy childhoods don't make cupcakes – they're probably successful investment bankers instead.'

What Vanessa did teach her, apart from the sauces, was how to make the most of ingredients, a skill learned from the post-war period of austerity in which Vanessa grew up. 'My mother could make the stringiest, toughest flesh – a bird that had been intensively farmed and frozen since the Ice Age – taste as if it were a lovingly reared poulet de Bresse,' she writes in *How to Eat*. Rationing was still in force until 1952, so cooks had to make the most of very few ingredients. You had to use your imagination. You learned that you had to slow-cook tough bits of meat, and grow herbs in your garden if you want to make the most out of simple ingredients. My mother would take a large tomato and stuff it with bread-crumbs and herbs and it would become a wonderfully moist and tasty centrepiece of a meal. Moneyed or not, this was the reality facing Vanessa and every other domestic goddess of the time.

Nigella and her sister Thomasina chopped and cooked, tasted and sniffed their way into a tight sisterly bond, while little Horatia, tottering six years behind, did not get much of a look in. 'I love having someone in the kitchen just to talk to as I chop and weigh and stir and generally get things ready,' Nigella writes in *How to Eat*. And perhaps as an acknowledgement of the support she misses from her sister who died of breast cancer in 1994, she adds, 'I love cooking with other people too. I do it rarely, though I used to often with my sister, Thomasina. There's something about that industrious intimacy that is both cushioning and comforting, but also hugely confidence-building. I love that sense of companionable bustle, of linked activity and joint enterprise. It makes it easier to attempt food that normally you would shrink from, not because you rely on another's capabilities or experience necessarily, but because you aren't isolated in the attempt.'

Horatia tries to take Thomasina's place, but the dynamic is just not the same. She appears in some of the TV programs, happy to be asked to the table, but on one occasion she is invited into the hot seat to chop and season, as her sister once did. Horatia is clearly uncomfortable with the role. 'Pepper?' she suggests. 'I would wait until the beef is browned first,' replies her big sister. Later she offers a culinary compliment: 'It's nice and gooey', to which Nigella snaps sarcastically, 'Thanks a *lot*.' Nigella takes over, obviously not happy with the way it's done, and although she's obviously the head chef in her TV kitchen, doling out orders to her commis-chefs throughout the series, poor old Horatia looks crestfallen, as though this is the story of her life. She even lives in the house Nigella left behind, the TV home in Goldhawk Road with the ghosts of the Diamond days for company. When Olivia Lichentstein is compiling a list of quotes from those nearest to her for an article on the Domestic Goddess in *Eve* magazine, Horatia's sarcastically sums her sister up as 'overrated'.

Bruce Goodison, the director of the pilot for *Nigella Bites*, is still close to Horatia whom he met during the filming and went on to hire as his Assistant Producer on *Ruby Wax*. 'They're very similar, very charming,' he said. 'You can definitely tell that they're sisters.' She hasn't inherited the Salmon looks, and is smaller, feistier, punkier and less elegant than her sister, but, says Goodison, 'If you close your eyes you can't tell who's talking – they're very likely to come out with the same thing. She and Nigella live in the same world. They go on holiday together and have dinner together regularly.' Horatia is fiercely private about her life; when I rang to check a rumor she told me in no uncertain terms that her life is *not* in the public domain. 'Horatia doesn't want the fame, although she works in TV, so she loves to be around famous people,' said Bruce. As the youngest in the family and the only one who doesn't live in the spotlight, she subverts the Lawson image. 'She's the "bad girl" of the family,' Nigella's friend Christopher Silvester said. 'She smokes like a chimney and dresses in a kind of punky way. She's got a very irreverent sense of humour too.'

Nigella doesn't know if her mother was bulimic or anorexic – food disorders weren't identified so clearly in those days – but recognizes now that she became a 'pusher', making her children eat. 'When I was very small you stayed at the table until you'd eaten everything,' she told Sue Lawley. Mealtimes, she said, were torture. 'You sat and ate what you were given, and if you didn't you were made to sit there until you did or have it served up congealed for the next meal,' she told the *Guardian*. Nigella used the little power that children have by refusing to eat, and she remembers being at that table for four hours on one terrible evening. Imagine the steely conflict between beautiful, thin mother and defiant daughter determined not to get fat.

She is convinced that she became a cook to gain control over food and to get her own back for those terrible tea times. 'Cooking,' she told the *Guardian*, 'is actually quite aggressive and controlling and sometimes, yes, there is an element of force-feeding going on. So I like to cook, I like to have people round my table, eating my food, and sometimes I feel it come over me. I find I'm staring at their plates, checking what they're eating and not eating, and then I can't help myself and this hectoring tone comes out, "Oh, are you not having any of the chard?" or, "Is something wrong with the crepe?" I wish I wouldn't do that.'

Thomasina was sixteen months her junior and quite the opposite in character. 'She wasn't like Dominic and me at all. She was upbeat and practical.' Her brother told the *Sunday Times Magazine* that he and Nigella were boarders at separate schools and it was not until she was fourteen and he was seventeen that they discovered each other. 'Nigella didn't speak much and was very withdrawn and shy and unsure of herself. Suddenly she was a ravishing beauty. I came back from boarding school and in the space of a day saw what had happened. It was quite extraordinary.'

Dominic was a serious child, a boy-genius with what his extended family remember as limited social graces, and what Nigella calls a 'glorious Gothic imagination'. She remembers his reaction to Thomasina cutting her foot: 'He held a glass underneath to catch all the blood and placed it high on a windowsill to attract plenty of toothy vampires.' Later he would take Nigella under his wing, remembering perhaps how people had responded to his mother's show-stopping beauty. 'She would go to parties and say nothing, and be completely passive, and everyone would just stand and stare at her as if at an incredible object,' he said of Nigella. 'I was concerned that people, including Nigella, might under-estimate her considerable intellect.' Nigella would later prove that it is the observers of life who often work out how to play the game faster than their peers.

At Oxford, where Dominic had already blazed a trail for her, she adopted the bluestocking mask of specs, an over-ripe figure and political and literary rhetoric which Dominic says he preferred to the silent beauty package. 'I thought it was more interesting for her,' he said protectively. 'What's remarkable is that she's now harmonized these two parts – the bluestocking and the glamour girl. She can bring down the house with drop-dead good looks and have an intellectu-ally fierce argument without fear.'

Her big brother still has dinner with her most Friday nights, and although he was until recently a high-powered newspaper editor renowned for his fierce intellect, and what Nigella calls a 'genetic predisposition to pomposity with unspeakable dress sense', he slips easily into babying his sister. 'It always amazes people if he's having a serious conversation with them that I can arrive and he'll drop that snappy interrogator's voice and start talking to me in a babyish pigeon-like coo. He calls me LaLa and playfully starts plaiting my hair. People simply cannot believe it.'

By the mid-1970s, Sir Freddie Ayer, philosopher and wit, had begun to offer a distraction that would polarize the family, although it would take until the 1979 Conservative election victory for the divorce to be finalized. Sir Freddie provided the love and adoration that Vanessa craved. With Vanessa happier, the family atmosphere was calmer, and the beginnings of a new relationship between mother and eldest daughter could emerge. 'I think that when she met Freddie Ayer, she settled down,' Alan Watkins said. She and Sir Freddie met at one of the many salons held by their mutual friend, Margot Walmsley, the editor of *Encounter* magazine, while he was a Professor of Philosophy at Oxford University. 'You could set your clock by Vanessa's arrival on the afternoon train,' laughed Sir Peregrine, who was a regular guest at their many parties. 'He adored her. He thought she was decorative and very sweet. Everyone loved going there and being with the two of them. She was so lively and flirtatious. She was very witty and would make very mischievous observations about people that made us all laugh.'

Nigel Lawson had already turned to his secretary, Therese Maclear, for solace, and in 1976, just as Nigella was finding her feet at Godolphin and Latymer, Therese and Nigel announced that they were to have a baby. Emily Lawson-Tancred says that although it was 'a surprise' when Tom was born, Nigella seemed 'to take it in her stride'. This was a teenager not known for her easy-going nature, who was about to tackle her A Levels, whose parents were both having affairs. Yet Emily, who spent every lunchtime with her, said that she didn't talk about it much. 'It's amazing what you take for granted when you're a child. Her family were very forward-thinking compared to a lot of our friends. Her mother was with Freddie Ayer, but I would go for tea and it would all seem very normal. Her mother would be in the kitchen just like anyone's mother would be.'

While the atmosphere was icy for much of the time, it was also intellectual and often pugnacious as the young Lawsons grew up. Dominic has spoken of his tendency to bully, a 'real intellectual thuggishness' and his 'glee in squashing people who really deserve it'. With Nigel debating economics in one corner, and Freddie discussing logical positivism, honing his thoughts on his version of the verification principle (an attempt at creating a process for determining whether a sentence has any logical meaning), you'd think that there would have been plenty of opportunity to sharpen their own wits.

Nigella doesn't remember it that way at all. A left-wing liberal, the young Nigella had 'the occasional political fit at my dad', as she told Andrew Harrison. 'He would say, "It's quite right that you should think those things at your age," which drove me mad. The funny thing is that my father is a very confident person and – maybe it's a Jewish thing – we come from a family where there's lots of talk and debate. He would never have wanted us not to argue with him. He wanted us to say why we thought what we thought, rather than just say "You fascist bastard", but there was no sense in which one was expected to have a view. Also, he didn't talk about politics very much. In families you don't, because the politics within the family are far more interesting. You don't talk shop.'

Confidence too was not in short supply among the Lawson role models. Even at seventy-seven years old, Sir Freddie was big enough to take on Mike Tyson, whom he considered to be harassing Naomi Campbell at a party. He asked Tyson to stop, to which Tyson replied, 'Do you know who the fuck I am? I'm the heavyweight champion of the world.' Freddie is said to have barely raised an eye as he retorted, 'And I am the former Wykeham Professor of Logic. We are both pre-eminent in our field; I suggest that we talk about this like rational men.'

Her relationship with her mother was thawing as both women grew up. 'She was much closer to her when she was a teenager and just before she died,' remembered Nigella's friend, Emily. 'Vanessa wasn't a great mother to young children. She was so young herself.' And Nigella's relationship with her father, now happily sitting just where he had always wanted to be – at Thatcher's side – was extremely close. 'She adored her father,' said Emily. 'She was unbelievably fond of him. They used to listen to music together and talk a lot. I remember when we were at school, she would wait up for him to come home from the House of Commons just so they could talk. Nigella confessed that she worshipped him in the way most little girls do.'

Nigel and Therese were married in 1979 after the election that first brought Margaret Thatcher to power and Nigel into government as Financial Secretary to the Treasury. Nigella blamed Therese for the break-up in her family, and it was many years before she would forgive her. 'I was nineteen, and at that age you're not the best judge of people,' she said. 'You think you know everything and you know nothing. But she's made my father very happy and now I adore her. They have two incredibly nice, lovely children and I always say to my father, "God knows that can't be your doing." '

Therese certainly seemed to have found the humanity in this 'pompous' (Vanessa) and 'absent' (Nigella) father figure, and his emotional remoteness was nowhere to be seen when in 1981 he witnessed the birth of his second child with Therese, Emily, the first time he said he'd been anywhere near the sharp end. The family has now moved to France, but Nigella is pleased that he finally seems to notice who and what she is. At a lunch after she and Charles Saatchi moved in together, he told her what every daughter wants to hear. 'How happy the children are,' he told her. 'And that's a great credit to you.' 'That's the furthest he'll go,' she says. 'He's not someone who likes emotional conversations.'

CHAPTER THREE

Uovo purgatorio and yards of tulle

Nigella's first taste of freedom came when she and Emily Lawson-Tancred set off for Italy after Nigella had taken her Oxbridge exams. It was February 1979, and they were heading for Florence to learn Italian, live off uovo purgatorio (eggs baked en cocotte with tomatoes), and nurture a love of all things Italian that would influence so much of the rest of her life. 'We had both been working to save up for the trip,' Emily said. 'I think she had a job in Monsoon or something. We flew to Pisa and then got a flat in the center of Florence. We shared a chambermaid job and did alternate mornings, which gave us plenty of time to have fun.'

Nigella wrote about their time there in *How to Eat*. 'I first had salsa verde when I was a chambermaid in Florence. I was there with a schoolfriend and we used to go most evenings, to a trattoria called Benvenuto and eat tortellini in brodo, their penne al modo nostro which involved an intensely garlicky tomato sauce, then moussey-sweet fegato, or my favourite, tongue with salsa verde. Now I wonder how good the restaurant was, but then, when most of the time we were living on a bottle of wine, a loaf of bread and a kilo of tomatoes between us a day, it seemed like Heaven. Anyway, after a while, we came back mostly for the clientele, made up in significant part by the local community of transsexuals and transvestites. The most beautiful of all of them, and the one generally held to be the glorious and burnished figure-head, the presiding force and icon, was a Bardot-esque blonde, only more muscular, known as La Principessa; those less appreciative of her construction referred to her simply as La Romana. I felt I'd arrived when she huskily called out "Ciao bella" to me across the street one day.'

Nigella decided to take a short course to improve her spoken Italian at Perugia University, which offered courses for foreign students. Cramming an Italian O Level and A Level in two years at Godolphin and Latymer had proved that she was a very good linguist, but it wasn't just the language that so impressed Nigella with Italy. 'She loved the Italian way of life, the humor, the food, the way everyone was so relaxed about it all,' Emily said.

She and Emily would pack their bags and head back to Italy as often as they could, staying with friends like Sarah Johnson who had borrowed a house from her family's friend, the sculptor Henry Moore. It was the summer of 1980 when they piled into what Sarah calls Moore's 'rather suburban house. A lot of our friends had turned up their noses at first when they realized it wasn't a Tuscan villa.' As often happens with student holidays in someone else's home, they had to call in a local plumber. 'Along came this rather surly man who, when he saw Nigella, absolutely melted,' Sarah said. 'Men did react when they saw her. We're all so used to seeing pictures of beautiful women that when you see Nigella she somehow upsets all your previous convictions of what beautiful women should look like. But she doesn't threaten women. Around women with thin thighs you can feel lower than low, but Nigella does have rather hefty thighs and you can feel positively endorsed when you're around her. She was never what I would call big boned, though – if you look at her ankles and wrists, you can see that her structure is quite delicate. She has Nigel's metabolism and Vanessa's bone structure.'

Her first Italian summer left her barely enough time to pack her duffel coat and head up to the Ivory Towers of Oxford in the autumn of 1979, where she was to read medieval and modern languages at Lady Margaret Hall. Composer Julian Nott was in the year below, and remembers her as one of the most glamorous and best-known undergraduates. 'She was very beautiful. She really stood out in the crowd,' he said.

Rather embarrassingly for her, her father had just become Thatcher's Treasury Secretary in 1979, and would become Chancellor of the Exchequer by the time she left, and possibly because she recognized a shared background with the son of the Secretary of State for Trade at the time, Sir John Nott, she would invite Julian for tea. Their fathers had worked together on the economics team while the Conservatives had been in opposition. Nigel Lawson was yet to become the face of the 1980s, and it would be Julian's father who would be regularly on the television news from

1982, updating us about the latest from the Falklands War. Julian said that they did not discuss their fathers at all. This was before she began force-feeding her guests cupcakes and whipping up risottos for twenty, and an invitation for a cup of tea meant just a cup of tea. He remembers her as 'very sweet, very confident and self-assured, extremely kind and not at all snooty. Everyone liked her.'

Sarah Johnson was in the year above Nigella at Lady Margaret Hall, and they've remained friends ever since. She remembers her early days in the kitchen. 'She was among the first mixed cohort of men and women in the college, and they were spending lots of money on the Junior Common Room – there was a new bar and a dining room and a kitchen where you could entertain.' Nigella was one of the few students who would talk about food – ingredients, recipes, ideas – much to the amazement of people like Sarah. 'She would talk endlessly to Tracey [Schofield, daughter of a 'wonderful pastry-maker', according to Nigella in *How to Eat*] about the difference between St Ivel and Flora, or the benefits of walnut oil. They were the only ones who would discuss really sophisticated ingredients, and I'd think it was so boring.' Tracey went on to look after the cookery list at the publishing house, Faber.

Nigella cooked for her undergraduate mates too, practising new and old ideas until she became known as the Queen of Onion Soup. It was all about cooking with no money. According to Sarah, Nigella was doing a prototype of Heston Blumenthal in those days, and was experimenting with food coloring to dye foods. 'She was very into kitsch and decided to do something for Valentine's Day and so we made pink cheese straws using cochineal. We cooked batches and batches of these things, and they were awful. The cochineal had made them really bitter so you couldn't eat them, and they came out looking like pink worms with yellow blodges where the pastry hadn't quite taken the cochineal. I think Nigella and I ate the lot – no one else would touch them.'

By the age of twenty she was a large, buxom creature, shielding her guilt at her size with a curtain of raven hair. She was referred to as 'handsome' in the papers of the time, and it must have been galling when her father, whom she was barely speaking to anyway, lost five stone (Stone is a British unit of measurement equaling fourteen pounds) and wrote a best-selling diet book about it in 1996. ('The recipes were actually written by my stepmother,' Nigella said scathingly. 'As befits a diet book, it was a very slender volume.') Nigella really could eat for England. 'She was great to have around because she and I were both what you might call "hefty" women and loved to eat,' said Sarah. Nigella was never full. 'She really is extraordinarily greedy. I've seen her eat a bowl of pasta that was meant for ten people. She just starts at one end, and picks away while she's doing other things until it's all gone.'

She was joined at the hip at this time with two best friends. One was Nicky Shulman, soon to be a model, daughter of theater critic Milton Shulman and sister of *Vogue* editor Alexandra; the other was Domenica Fraser, daughter of Sir Ian, who would by the end of the decade be working on movies such as *Hellbound: Hellraiser II* before going on to support her husband, one of the original founders of the Ottakars chain of bookshops and Tory candidate for Ludlow in the 2005 election.

Nigella was part of the in-crowd, and loved to party. The difference between Nigella and her mates and the rest of the students of the 1980s was that the latter didn't have their party snaps delivered directly to their parents' breakfast tables via the newspapers. When the *Sunday Times Magazine* published a feature called 'Bright Young Things' in March 1981, showing the media princes and princesses at play, it revealed just what our would-be leaders get up to behind closed doors.

Journalist Jeremy Wayne followed society photographer Dafydd Jones to all the best parties and watched in amusement as the young snobs let their hair down. He commented, 'There was Katie Hick, daughter of His Excellency our ambassador to Ecuador, removing a young fellow's trousers and – good gracious – a buttock was exposed. And Nigella Lawson – wasn't she something to do with the Cabinet? – was snogging Guy Faber, a scion of the famous publishing family. And there was someone called Paul Golding, if you could believe it, in a dress. Yards and yards of brilliant white tulle, and oh, that disdainful look on his face. And no, surely that couldn't be – but, oh, it was – the Hon. Pandora Mond, daughter of society hostess Sonia Lady Melchett (now Lady Sonia Sinclair), in a shocking sheer black dress with a nipple exposed.'

Oxford University was divided into bizarre societies such as the Dangerous Sports Club, Piers Gaveston and the Assassins. Dafydd Jones was there at their parties – and Wayne was often by his side. 'He shot Charlie Cory-Wright wearing leopard-skin with his hand where it should not have been, namely sliding up Pandora Mond's skirt. He found

Jonathan Burnham (former head of Chatto & Windus and Nigella's editor on *How to Eat*), and Hughie Grant, unknown then, but pretty beyond belief – also in leopard-skin (I guess it was a look) – in stitches at a boys-only Gaveston dinner. He snapped musician and playwright, the Hon. Valentine Guinness, in taffeta and feathers and writer Paul Golding, founder of the exotic Kay White society, emerging from his finals in boxers and gold bangles.'

It was a far cry then from the world of the sullen teenager who hid from the outside world. 'I needed to be away from home and building my own life before I began to have a sense of myself,' explained Nigella. 'I began to be less shy as I moved away from the family unit. I was no longer constrained by my allotted character in the script – the over-sensitive flower.' 'Shy?' laughed one of her friends from Lady Margaret Hall. 'She wasn't shy. People who are shy don't get noticed or remembered, and she was certainly noticed and remembered.' This was a woman who was so self-assured that she would walk up to literary agent Ed Victor at one of these parties and tipsily announce to him that one day he would be her agent. 'I don't know who you are,' he is reported to have said (although he must have been the only person there who didn't), 'but I dare say you're right.'

'I wouldn't call her a socialite,' Dafydd Jones said. 'There were plenty of people who were at that time, but she wasn't. It's just that when she was around, she attracted a lot of attention because she was just so beautiful. I took lots of photographs at those parties and my camera was attracted to certain people. I remember taking lots of pictures of Hugh Grant too. You could see that he had something special.

Nigella had that too.' Hugh Grant, Julian Nott reminded me, had just appeared (he was then known as Hughie) in a low-budget Oxford Film Foundation movie called *Privilege* with fellow stars-to-be Imogen Stubbs and *The Fast Show*'s Mark Williams. With an unexpected amount of attention given to the high jinks of bed-hopping Oxford undergrads, Hugh had become a bit of a star. 'Hugh and Nigella were certainly the most glamorous and well-known faces around,' said Julian. 'She had a luminous quality,' said Sarah. 'She has always walked into a room and lit it up with her beauty.'

Even if she was surrounded, as she always had been, by power, money and influence (although this time as part of it rather than *apart* from it), Nigella was furiously independent and keen to make her own way in the world. Dafydd Jones remembers her first job at Clement's restaurant in Oxford. 'I had set up a photo for the *Sunday Times* of "Bright Young Things" from Oxford, and Nigella was among those chosen for the photo. Afterwards the journalist and I went to lunch, and Nigella was our waitress. Most of her contemporaries were driving around in fast cars, but Nigella was busy working to pay her way.'

Her boyfriends were all independently wealthy, and, said Sarah Johnson, followed a pattern. 'They were all highly intelligent and needed mothering. It was like they needed a domestic goddess of their own and looked to Nigella to provide that. She was only too happy to do it.' Nigella admitted as much. 'I joked that my greatest talent was turning a one-night stand into a three-year relationship, meaning I probably never got rid of those who should have just been a one-night stand.'

'She was always so maternal,' said Sarah. 'At the earliest age, she would always be looking into prams and cooing at babies. The only thing I remember her saying about her half-brother, Tom, was that he was really sweet. I remember thinking that I wouldn't be quite so generous under the circumstances.' Her men also adored her. When the novelist A. N. Wilson dedicated one of his novels to her, eyebrows were raised. 'He was certainly madly in love with her,' said Emily Lawson-Tancred, 'but I don't think they ever went out together.'

'John Diamond was the first boyfriend of hers I liked,' Sarah told me. 'He came from the rag trade and he'd been around a bit, and he didn't need looking after. Ironically, it turned out that he would need more looking after than any of them. She had been mothering all these men for years. Trav Morgan was one who was totally unworldly, although he was utterly single-minded. He announced aged twenty that he wanted a job selecting records on Radio 3, and that's exactly what he did. I remember he had to have six holes on each side of his handmade shoes. He had this kind of frightened deer quality about him – it was very Bambi. And then there was Alan Jenkins, who was a self-obsessed poet who was so in love with her.'

And there was Hubie Gibb, a barrister in the making who spent his weekends jumping off bridges on pieces of elastic, or skiing down mountain slopes hanging on to a grand piano, as part of Oxford's Dangerous Sports Club. One of the early bungee jumpers, he famously leapt off the Grand Canyon Bridge, the highest in the world, tied to a bungee rope. Hubie was an Old Etonian whose father was a Marshal of the Diplomatic Corps. 'Hubie Gibb was one of those men she used to look after,' sighed Sarah. 'He took his laundry, including his underpants and socks, to the dry cleaners for the whole of the first term at Oxford because he didn't know what else to do with them. I'm sure the dry cleaners had a field day. They probably put them in the washing machine and charged him the dry cleaning rate.' Emily Lawson-Tancred had a soft spot for him. 'Hubie Gibb was very good-looking, the classic English gentleman. He was an Old Etonian with a wonderful English understated humor. He was a very gentle man.'

Nigella is either a charmed woman, or someone who has a terrible run of luck, according to your half-empty or half-full position on life. She would soon be haunted by the deaths of her loved ones, yet it was her own life that was first in the balance. 'She was in a terrible car crash in Oxford in which she was nearly killed,' Sarah Johnson told me. 'She was coming back from a point-to-point meeting with about five people in the car. They were all drunk as lords, and the driver, Nicholas Kermack, lost control of the steering wheel.' Tragically, he died a year later of an asthma attack following a heavy student drinking session. 'Nigella was in and out of the Radcliffe [hospital] all term, and she had back problems for years afterwards, but she could so easily have lost her looks.' Emily Lawson-Tancred was sitting on Nigella's lap in the accident and broke the glass for her friend as the side of her head smashed the windscreen. She saved not only her own face but Nigella's from disfigurement. Although they were all merry, she rejects the idea that Nigella would have been drunk. 'She wasn't a drinker. She liked to be around drink, but she would always sip. She's always been able to stay in control. She's certainly not addictive. I remember that we used to smoke Moriarty cigarettes when we were in Italy, and she gave up just like that. I've never seen her taking drugs either. Dancing is how she lets her hair down.'

CHAPTER FOUR

Kaftans and Bloody Marys

Nigella left Oxford with a second-class honors degree, although had she not suffered the nightmare of turning over an exam paper to find that she hadn't read any of the books selected she might well have got a first. 'The exams were an absolute disaster for her because she found that she couldn't answer a single question on one of the papers,' said Sarah Johnson. 'I remember bumping into her at LMH [Lady Margaret Hall] and she was holding a bag of frozen spinach, and she told the story about the exam. She tore open the bag of spinach and ate the lot. I was absolutely amazed.'

Independent on Sunday columnist and former *Private Eye* journalist Christopher Silvester met Nigella when she came down from Oxford as one of the 'It Girls' milling around the London media pool, looking for a place on a newspaper. 'I invited her to a *Private Eye* lunch simply because I'd seen her photo and found her attractive,' he admitted. 'She was extraordinarily shy and really didn't say very much. She didn't have terribly good teeth and seemed rather self-conscious about them, though she's certainly got much nicer, shiny teeth now. Nevertheless, she was very beautiful, and I think her shyness made her even more appealing.'

This was 1983, and with her mother's face and her father's name Nigella was a spirit fighting to get out as she headed on to the world stage. By the time she left Oxford her father was a very recognizable figure as Margaret Thatcher's Chancellor of the Exchequer. Nigella remembered that as they settled in to their new jobs Thatcher told him there would have to be cuts, 'and the first is your hair'. She laughed. 'The idea of Mrs T being witty is almost alarming. In television your boss would also tell you to cut your hair. It's all showbiz, darling.'

It was assumed that the young graduate with almost the same name would follow in her father's footsteps. 'My mother said on her death bed,' Nigella told Cassandra Jardine in the *Sunday Telegraph*, 'that she would never have allowed the name had she known he would be so famous. But she must have known that he was that type. She also said that all the women in our family had four-hour labors. I cursed her for that too.' But Nigella was not going to play ball, and didn't even vote in her first possible election of 1979. 'I forgot to register,' she protested, but when asked said that she would never vote Tory, preferring a more SDP line to her father's.

Nigella was touchy when interviewed about her political beliefs throughout her father's period in government. 'I do feel I have to say what I think. I don't speak to my father every time I write,' she would tell Paul Davidson later. A friend of hers told him, 'She really isn't crazy about her dad, and her political views may be a kickback about everything that has happened in her family.' When a colleague whose own marriage was failing suggested to her that children fare better if their parents divorce when they are older, she told him, 'Absolutely not.' 'She was shattered when her father walked out,' he said.

Nigella preferred books to politics, and it was as part of the court of flamboyant Palestinian-born publisher Naim Attallah that she joined a band of bright young women from similarly privileged backgrounds living on about £5,500 a year at Quartet. Nigella joined Rebecca Fraser, daughter of Lady Antonia Fraser, Sabrina Guinness, Asquith's great grand-daughter, Virginia Bonham Carter, Prince Charles's old flame, Emma Soames, and a host of other well-connected young socialites on the editorial team. It was a tremendously creative place to learn about publishing, and Quartet was pushing the boundaries, publishing translations alongside English-language authors, and was the first publishing house to establish a Middle East and Africa list. Controversial titles were making Quartet's name, with books like Tony Clifton and Catherine Leroy's *God Cried* about the Israeli invasion of Lebanon, and Jonathan Dimbleby and Donald McCullin's *The Palestinians* as well as novels by then-unknowns, Amin Maalouf, Tahar Ben Jelloun, Naguib Mahfouz and Hanan al-Shaykh. The list was unusual enough in itself as Georgia de Chamberet, who would do Nigella's job some years later, explained. 'What was even more unusual was that Quartet was publishing them alongside authors like Julian Barnes, Dennis Potter, Maeve Binchy, Alethea Hayter, Diana Athill, Elizabeth Wurtzel, Derek Jarman and Philip Mansel.' With sexy photographers like Helmut Newton, Bob Carlos Clarke and John Swannell launching their stunning illustrated books with Quartet too, this was considered the most exciting publishing house in town.

'There was a very special atmosphere which I don't think anyone has really managed to convey so far,' said Quartet's sales and marketing man, David Elliott, who worked with Nigella as 'a kind of apparatchik who took the girls to the parties'. He explained what set Quartet apart. 'Naim was twenty-five years ahead of his time. We were the first to publish Anaïs Nin in the UK and a list of forgotten American writers as well as Scandinavian writers that other people weren't even looking at at the time.'

Nigella brought a European dimension to the list. 'Her background was in modern languages, and she was very active in getting books like Bassani's *The Garden of the Finzi-Continis* on board. All the girls were very active. Naim had a talent for giving people their head. If someone really wanted to go with an idea for a book, and it made economic sense in Naim's odd way of making things make economic sense, he would let them. And once he'd made that decision, he stood by them, and took full public responsibility for it. That's probably why I could do a book about the political writings of Paul Robeson – which I think sold about seven copies. He can be a monster, but he is also incredibly generous.'

'It was a very creative, free environment, which you just don't get in publishing these days,' agreed Georgia de Chamberet, who was another of Attallah's well-connected editors. 'Publishing used to be about eccentrics, but it's become very corporate these days. People like Jubby Ingrams [the late daughter of *Private Eye*'s Richard Ingrams] couldn't have existed in the publishing world today. She was the queen of marketing at Quartet and a fabulous character with a very mischievous streak.'

Editorial director Stephen Pickles collaborated with Georgia de Chamberet in building up the European list into a memorable legacy some years after Nigella had left Quartet. But Quartet and Naim Attallah will be best remembered for the parties. Attallah was raising the profile of the company in ways previously unseen in the old-fashioned world of publishing and changing its shape for ever. 'He had a lot of business savvy,' said David. 'He injected capital but also brought a totally different PR dimension to publishing. We managed to get the company name into *Tatler* and Londoner's Diary every time we threw a party.'

This was when the publishing world was much more conservative than it is now, and held discreet launch parties, leaving the brasher parties to the mass media. Attallah managed to bridge the gap for the first time with his launch for Janet Reger's *Chastity in Focus* at what would become the Pineapple Dance studios in Covent Garden. Brian Clarke, famous for his stained-glass art, designed the party, and it was a spectacular event never seen before from such a highbrow publisher. 'We had girls walking around and serving canapés in Janet Reger lingerie,' said David. 'It was all a bit uncomfortable at first because there were lots of the older publishing crowd there who didn't know what to do, but it quickly became very lively.'

Needless to say, the party hit the headlines in the papers, and Attallah had set a new standard in publishing. 'You only have to look at *ES* magazine [the London *Evening Standard*'s weekly celebrity color supplement] to see what he started,' said David. Georgia de Chamberet, now director of the select writers' agency, Bookblast, remembers the parties as 'fabulously rumbustious, totally wild. I went to one in Soho just after I'd joined Quartet, and walked into a place filled with tiger skins and mirrors everywhere. They were very avant garde.' She remembers the launch of Naim's book *Women* at the Victoria and Albert Museum, which had been draped in blue crushed velvet. 'He'd brought in one of those moving statues that you see all over the place now, which was entrancing all the guests – who'd all had quite a skinful. There was one party where one of the guests was supposed to have peed on Naim's head, but I missed that one.'

If parties are about networking, Nigella, already fully equipped with what David Elliott called 'an innate ability to read the English social scene', was learning her art from the leader of the pack. Elliott described her as ambitious only in that she was sharp enough to know that there were opportunities all around her, and with the cream of the newspapers' literary critics sipping champagne with her at the Quartet parties, it was only a matter of time before she would make her next move.

The way into newspapers is often a sneaky one: start as a sub-editor, make friends, grab an opportunity to fill in for someone who's off sick, and shine wherever possible with your wit and enthusiasm. The route from Oxford University to Wapping is lined with a well-trodden red carpet, and Nigella's parents, particularly her mother, had eased her passage into the world of publishing and the media with the help of her own exceptional contacts from the youngest age.

Andrew Neil, an old family friend, was at the helm of the *Sunday Times*. But if it seemed that she was given a leg up into the chair of the deputy literary editor, in reality it wasn't quite that easy.

Nigella started off at the *Sunday Times* as an assistant in serializations in 1984. 'It was a pretty lowly job for someone like her,' said one of her bosses there. 'There were those who'd think that she'd be rather grand. In my recollection she was nothing of the sort. Someone as beautiful and clever as her who came from such a privileged background, you'd think that she would put on airs and graces, but she really didn't do that at all. In fact I always found her terribly nervous and lacking in confidence.'

'My most powerful memory of her is that she was very quiet,' said Ivan Fallon, now chief executive of the *Independent*, and then deputy editor of the *Sunday Times*. 'She would sit there with her long hair over her face, and didn't really talk to anyone. She kept herself very much to herself. She was very introverted, very different to the Nigella we see now.' Fallon said that she was very, very bright – a serious intellectual. 'She absolutely thrived in the books section although she was very junior there. She was a very young twenty-four-year-old.'

Nigella was introverted for a good reason: she had other things on her mind. Her mother had been diagnosed with liver cancer, and would die within a short period in 1985. 'She adored her stepfather and was worried about him too,' said Fallon. 'I think she was very preoccupied.'

Nigella was twenty-five when her mother died, at forty-eight. Nigella had just begun to have the kind of relationship with her mother that she had always wanted. Psycho-therapists say that more people blame their mothers for their unhappy lives than anyone else, and that it takes a great deal to let that go. But when her mother told Nigella that the cancer and inevitability of death provided her finally with some peace, an end to the worries that plagued her life, it wasn't what her newly compassionate daughter wanted to hear. 'I was so hurt by her not minding dying and leaving us,' she told Lynda Lee-Potter in the *Mail*. 'I found that difficult. And it seemed so unfair that I'd had such a short time when we'd become close. She thought I was the one in the family least able to cope, which seems strange considering how things have turned out.'

'When her mother died it was her first big bereavement, but she seemed to take it more easily in her stride than other people might have done,' said Sarah Johnson. 'It must have been quite shattering, but she carried on. I don't think she stopped being a young woman around town.' By day, the often overwhelming world of the *Sunday Times*, and by night, research for her *Spectator* restaurant column, for which she had just begun writing a fortnightly piece, were suitably distracting. She and Thomasina looked after their stepfather. 'It was a terrible illness,' remembered Peregrine Worsthorne. 'She and Freddie were so happy.' He remembers 'one of the sisters, Thomasina, probably', looking after Sir Freddie after Vanessa had gone. 'Margot Walmsley (who introduced the couple) would come round to his flat and leave cooked chicken wings in the fridge for him, but when he went to get one out for his supper he would often find that Thomasina had got there first.'

Nigella surrounded herself with her mother's things, collecting and hoarding her possessions as if memories alone were too fragile to hold on to. She and Thomasina spent as much time as they could together, chopping and cooking through the dark days until they had restored each other. They cooked Nursery Fish Pie on the evening after their mother died, and Nigella would include the recipe later in her book *Feast* in a chapter called 'Funeral Feast'. 'I don't think anyone wants to cook in the immediate shock of bereavement, and in my experience you are anyway unlikely to need something like an over-ordered Chinese takeaway, but a few days on cooking can be a calming act, and since the mind knows no rest and has no focus, the body may as well be busy. Or you may be making this for others in need.'

'Together we ate bowls of chicken broth with leeks and boiled potatoes,' Nigella said in *How to Eat*; 'roast chicken and leeks in white sauce with boiled potatoes; spaghettini with tomato sauce and lots of fresh basil on top.' Thomasina, an occupational therapist, had moved to Wales, and Nigella loved to hole up with her for weekend visits there or to play host to her sister in her own London flat. 'On the evening of her arrival, at the beginning of any weekend she stayed with me, we always shared taramasalata with warm pitta, alongside on the table a plate of hot crisp grilled bacon and a bunch of spring onions.'

She remembers how well-meaning people would ask how she was coping and, by way of empathetic consolation, tell her how well they remembered the sad death of a puppy. 'The mourning process,' she told Sally Vincent in the *Guardian*, 'is not a matter of universal understanding. We cross the road when the widow walks by because we do not know what to say. We are embarrassed by her grief. We say, "Oh, she has taken it well," with admiration, meaning you can hardly tell she's just suffered a bit of a setback. We use these ridiculous expressions – "Draw a line under it." "Go on with your life." "Put it all behind you." '

She may have become closer to her mother before she died, but relations with her father were still frosty, and they didn't improve in their grief. Ivan Fallon was a friend of Nigel's, having worked with him as City Editor on the *Sunday Telegraph* when Nigel had been Deputy Editor there, and remembered Nigella coming to him at the *Sunday Times* to ask if he was going to her father's Christmas party. 'She wasn't speaking to her father at the time,' he told me. 'I said I was, so she asked me if I would mind taking some presents for her half brother and sister. So I turned up at No. 11 Downing Street with a bag of presents.'

Ironically, despite the silence between the two, it was the economic conditions produced by her father's chancellorship that would give her her next big break on the road to super-stardom.

Nigel Lawson became the longest-running Chancellor of the Exchequer since David Lloyd George until Gordon Brown took the lead in September 2003. As Thatcher's Chancellor he created an economic climate in which champagne glasses were clinking around the wine bars and sushi restaurants of the City, and a new generation of young bucks grew up chanting Thatcher's mantra of looking out for number one. Cash-starved as Nigella and her friends were, they still managed to spend half their Sundays at Le

Caprice eating Eggs Benedict and getting through pitcher after pitcher of Bloody Marys, as she would later confess in her *Vogue* column.

Socialism was kicked into the gutter in the London of the 1980s, and despite Thatcher's belief that there was no such thing as 'society' a new sort of society was rising quickly from the ashes of the seventies, built on aspiration, wealth and greed. This was a soulless, thrusting world, the Yuppy Britain where everything was big and showy, and based on little more than hot air. Big shoulder pads, big hair, big cars and big expense accounts were propping up a new wave of chic *nouvelle cuisine* with tiny portions perched delicately on enormous plates. It was the decade in which there *was* such a thing as a free lunch, and the economic architect's daughter and future sons-in-law were networking their way right into the inner circle.

Sexy young chefs were earning small fortunes and hitting headlines in a country that wasn't yet selling olive oil in supermarkets (my mother was still getting hers from Boots). This was a world where the young Marco Pierre White, the first British chef ever to be awarded three Michelin stars, was able to charge £100 a head at Harvey's, while throwing customers on to the street if they dared to ask for extra pepper. Gary Rhodes was schmoozing the rich old ladies of Mayfair at the Greenhouse with his spiky hair and braised oxtail, and Jamie Oliver was but an eight-year-old helping out in the kitchen at his parents' Essex pub.

Eating out anywhere other than the local Italian, Indian, Chinese or wine bar had until now been the preserve of the rich. Now with the average middle-class wallet beginning to bulge, certainly in London and the big cities, chefs were becoming big business. The fathers of London's new restaurant scene, Nico Ladenis at Chez Nico, Albert Roux at Le Gavroche, Anton Edelman at the Savoy, Pierre Koffman at La Tante Claire and Raymond Blanc at Le Manoir aux Quat' Saisons in Oxford, were mentoring a new breed of chef whose sights were set on much more than their port reduction. Celebrity was something they could smell among the vanilla pods and fresh dill as new yuppy superstars chose to court the media on the steps of their favourite restaurants.

Nigella was one of the few members of her generation who really knew about food, and she watched this gastro-revolution with interest. She was only twenty-five when in 1985 she spotted a gap for a restaurant review column in the *Spectator* which would propel her to food stardom over the next fifteen years. Charles Moore, who later invited her into the *Daily Telegraph*, gave her a job at the *Spectator*. 'He asked me if I would contribute something to the magazine,' she wrote in a column for Moore in the *Telegraph* almost ten years later. 'As a young, not-quite journalist, I realized that I couldn't exactly tell him that I had no idea of what I could write, so I studied one issue of the magazine for two weeks, and then came back to him telling him that the readers were obviously affluent and it was ridiculous that there was no restaurant column. Think of the advertising revenue he would get from it, I encouraged him. He suggested we meet for lunch to discuss it and asked me to name a happening place. I couldn't. But we met and I did the job for twelve years. I don't think he ever got more than about two ads from it, but I enjoyed myself.'

As with all new jobs, the seas were not always calm, and the tabloids were ready and waiting to pounce on the daughter of the Chancellor at the first sign of a slip. In a rare story of Nigella throwing her weight around, the normally self-deprecating journalist had a run in at Chez Nico with Nico's wife Dinah-Jane. Nico Ladenis is seen by many of the great London chefs as the godfather of modern cuisine, and was the only self-taught chef in the world to have been awarded three Michelin stars for his restaurant on Park Lane. According to the tabloids, Nico himself accused Nigella of failing to make the grade as a food reviewer and being unable to identify accurately the ingredients in the dish she ate.

Nigella was earning a pittance compared with what she would be commanding a few years on, but it took a while for her to realize that it wasn't her bank balance that she had in common with her readership at the *Spectator*. 'Going out to restaurants is so expensive these days that I'm surprised people even think of going to places they don't know. So much safer to stick to old favourites where you know that you'll like it,' she wrote in her first column for the magazine. This was the world of Oxbridge and the celebrity heavyweights she knew so well. She could write clangers like: 'The problem with barbecues is the fear of being thought lower-middle-class,' without so much as an editor's question mark in the margin. This cushioned world of privilege wasn't yet making her rich, but she was unlikely to find out much about how the other half lived, although she did manage the occasional trip outside London to review a restaurant. She was usually less than impressed – unless she was visiting the handful of influential provincial restaurants such as the Walnut Tree in Abergavenny where Franco Taruschio was quietly changing the face of British cuisine. 'For us metropolitan types, there used to be just two reasons for venturing into the suburbs,' she wrote in the *Spectator* in 1990. 'The first was to watch football matches and the second was to commune with the spirit of John Betjeman and laugh at all those net curtains.'

It got worse. 'Do deputy managing directors (export) and accounting execs who have these places on their driveways appreciate what they're eating?' she asked her readers. 'Do they know how good it is, or how long the chef has spent overseeing the chopping and shredding of those baby vegetables for them to burst springlike on the tongue? Wouldn't they really prefer a well-done steak and a glass of Blue Nun in the local Berni?' And worse: 'You will know, however, that I am not that kind of snob, and so I didn't allow myself to be put off by the marbled wallpaper or the stippling, dragging or rag-rolling on the paintwork (though I think I shall scream if I ever see another paint effect again) nor was my enjoyment marred by the fact that the little Turner prints around the dining room were a) little Turner prints around the dining room and b) twinned with table arrangements provided by pastel-tinted, gyp-filled vases.'

Her regal nature was encouraged by her brother, who took over as editor of the *Spectator* during her time there. Dominic protected his sister from *hoi poloi* whenever he could and was known to treat her as a princess. A foreign correspondent told me what it was like to be on the receiving end. 'I was giving a dinner to my neighbours who were diplomats and keen on food, plus Alan Davidson, the former Ambassador to

Laos and father of food history in this country – he co-founded the annual Oxford Food Symposium at St Anthony's and later edited the *Oxford Companion to Food*. I very vaguely knew Nigella from her time working with Naim Attallah and had again met her at a party, so rang her to invite her to dinner with the above people. I think the dinner was on a Thursday or a Friday. Suddenly on Monday I received a call from Dominic Lawson who introduced himself on the telephone and then asked me to explain the purpose of the dinner and why I had invited his sister. I mumbled something vague about mutual interest in food, at which he seemed to be satisfied and then said Nigella would be in touch, which she was and ended up coming to the dinner. Any thought of seeing her again was somewhat dashed when I read her *Spectator* review of Stephen Bull's new restaurant off Marylebone High Street, which I had recommended to her. She said something like a friend had recommended it but she thought it was rather indifferent so she probably should change her restaurant selections or maybe just change her friends.'

The common touch was not something she had mastered, nor ever wished to, as David Edgar, the producer of *Nigella Bites* and *Forever Summer*, explained. 'I do populist TV, and there were times when I would worry about her vocabulary. She'd want to talk about being an empiricist rather than a theorist in the way that she cooks and I'd say, "Do you think we can talk about empiricism on a cookery program?" and she'd say, "Absolutely." There were times when I would question how accessible she was being, and she would take the view that this is her unique approach. It turned out that she was absolutely right.'

According to the *Daily Mail*, she was sacked from Talk Radio in 1995, the station that launched the 'shock jock' in the UK, for casually dropping in the fact that she didn't do her own shopping. In the days when home delivery was reserved for the well heeled, Nigella's gaffe on her breakfast show, on which she was supposed to be chatting about make-up and men with her listeners, didn't go down well with the station controllers, who considered that her lifestyle 'did not fit in with the average listener'. Nappy Express, which delivered heavy baby items and household products to Nigella's door for a minimum order of £20, couldn't have known that within ten years home delivery would be one of the most popular ways of shopping.

While Nigella was wooing a rich and powerful – and largely Tory – readership at the *Spectator*, her confidence was growing. It was time to move up. The Wapping strike of 1986 offered Nigella the opportunity for her next career move within the *Sunday Times*, and for someone claiming at the time to be politically left of center, the way she did it showed early signs of the mover and shaker she would become. It was a defiant move. 'It was the time of great change in Fleet Street,' remembered a colleague on the *Sunday Times*. 'Murdoch took on the printing unions and moved his papers from Fleet Street and other sites to the new plant at Wapping which was surrounded by razor wire. The National Union of Journalists sided with the printers and ordered the strike, so it was down to individual choice as to who crossed the picket line. Nigella was one of the ones who did.'

The Literary Editor of the paper, Claire Tomalin, had decided not to go with her staff to Wapping. 'She declined,

saying it was too right-wing and too down-market for her,'
said one of her colleagues, so it was her deputy Penny Perrick
who crossed the line to step into her shoes. 'It was all hands
on deck just to get the paper out,' said her colleague, 'and
Nigella went too. Once she was there, Penny gave her the job
of Deputy Literary Editor.' Ivan Fallon was Deputy Editor of
the *Sunday Times* and remembered the moment. 'We were
standing in the newsroom and I looked at Penny and said,
"Right, you're Literary Editor now, and Nigella, you're the
deputy." We were all so preoccupied with other things at that
time that everyone just got on with it.'

Nigella hadn't reckoned on the response from the chapel of
her own union, the National Union of Journalists, who called
an hour-and-a-half meeting to discuss this young whipper-
snapper. David Lipsey, father of the chapel at the *Sunday
Times*, explained 'Complaints have been made about her
qualifications. To be offered a job on the *Sunday Times* you
have to have worked for three years in the provinces or on a
weekly, or have specialist qualifications for the job. A vote
among the ninety chapel members to go into dispute over the
matter and to take industrial action was rejected by a mere
three votes, although there were also a number of absten-
tions.' The decision was made that as a member of the NUJ
she should go off and get some more training while retaining
her part-time job at the *Sunday Times*. 'We didn't want to
chuck her out of the building,' said Lipsey, 'but we decided not
to stick to the letter of the law.' None of her colleagues seems
to remember much about the training she was told to do, and
several said they could rattle off a list of influential journalists and editors who had also bypassed the provinces on their

road to Wapping. As Deputy Editor, Nigella's job was more administrative and editorial than journalistic, and perhaps she could put one of her first literary interviews down as training. It was with Arthur Miller.

'I don't know why she got the interview with Arthur Miller,' said one of her bosses. 'Maybe someone thought that he would respond better to her than a male journalist. But she was very nervous about it. You'd have thought that someone with her intelligence would have more confidence, but I remember she said to me, "How do I interview him? What do people want to know about him?" I told her that she should ask him what Marilyn Monroe was like in bed. And she said, "Do people really want to know about that? I can't ask him that. This is a great literary figure." I told her that he probably wouldn't reply anyway. To her credit, when she came back she said that she had asked him. He hadn't replied. Of course she could have been fibbing, but I don't think she was. She really went up in my estimation. It was a literary interview so she wasn't under instructions to do so. It was a ballsy thing to do.'

'I was always trying to encourage her to write,' said Fallon. 'I wanted her to do a column. She was a very good sub-editor, but she wasn't very ambitious. She never gave the impression that she was very interested in writing more. She might have written some book reviews, but other than that, not very much at all. It's possible that she was very nervous about her ability to write. She was a well-known name and she knew a lot of people, so I wanted to give her the chance.'

She wasn't quite so reserved in her column at the *Spectator*, where her florid prose and salivating descriptions over the past year were beginning to get her noticed. 'I never realized that it was so hard to write about food until she went on holiday and I thought it'd be fun if Tariq Ali stepped in,' wrote her brother, the latest editor of the *Spectator*. 'He had a go but rang back saying it was virtually impossible. Describing the sensual is far trickier than anyone imagines.'

A job as Literary Editor at the *Sunday Times* should have been a dream for a young journalist finding her way on the streets of London, but it wasn't all roses. 'I didn't want to be an executive, being paid to worry rather than think,' she said. 'You either freelance in your home life *or* your work life.' After two years in the job, she looked into her little black book and found herself a job as a columnist for the *Evening Standard*.

A fellow columnist on the *Standard* at the time, Peter McKay, remembers her as a 'spectral, ethereal figure' who rarely came in to the office. He described her columns as 'schoolgirl essays'. 'It was the name that the paper wanted,' he said 'although I've never understood why Lawson was such a great name. I've never thought Nigel Lawson was a hugely well-regarded character yet somehow the name meant something and she wrote for the *Standard* for a long time. Her column was just her thinking out loud. She seemed always frightened to take a point of view.' He was amazed that she went on to write for the *Observer*. 'It's just marketing,' he said.

The chief sub-editor at the *Evening Standard*, Peter Jessop, remembered that Genevieve Cooper was Deputy Editor at the time, and was behind the decision to bring her in as a columnist. 'She was always keen on people with connections,' he said. Peter said his team of subs remembered her copy as 'horrendous. They had their heads in their hands for much of time. With most columnists you know at least what they are trying to say, but with Nigella you just didn't have a clue.' Her 1,000-word column would have to be reworked by the subs until it hung together. 'Columnists are hired for their writing skills. You feel that it's not your function to turn their words into great columns. If you're working on a news story or with someone who's not a professional writer, there is a feeling of achievement when you can turn it round, but you resent it if they're earning a wage as a columnist with a nice big picture next to their byline.' Peter said she didn't seem to have much to write about in the first place. 'We were struggling to see what she was trying to say. There was a definite sigh of relief when she moved on. Nobody would have said that she had mastered the art of writing during her time at the *Standard*.'

Ask any sub and he or she will tell you tales of looking through the copy of the big-name columnists and scratching their heads. 'We'd sit back and say, "OK, what shall So-and-So say this week, then?" It's the biggest grief among the subs. We're seen as the down-table drones who will make a piece work, while the columnists are the people with the names, the cash, the plaudits.' Peter Jessop said that some of the big names even ring up to ask what they should write about that week. 'She probably did improve with experience,' he said kindly, although not at the *Standard*. 'She was a bit like Emma Soames, who was terrible at first and then really did become a very good writer.'

But if she had difficulty structuring a theme at the time, at least she was pleasant. 'It's a great asset in this business,' Peter said. 'Some of the better writers are crusty old curmudgeons.' She was also attractive. 'She wasn't glamorous at all when she came in, and then you'd see her at a party in the evening and she'd have turned into a stunner.'

Perhaps the feedback from her media colleagues might have encouraged her to sharpen her wit, and she soon attracted the attention of the tabloids for accusing her father's boss of being paranoid and vengeful in her *Standard* column in 1989. Nigella described Mrs Thatcher's 'obsession' with the Spycatcher case and then Europe as 'well and truly in the grip of paranoia. In what seems to be an increasingly private battle against Brussels, she has made it startlingly apparent that she is much happier for the United Kingdom to become the 51st state rather than a mere member country of the EC ... The fact is that Mrs Thatcher doesn't like being a European, and you can only presume from her advertising campaign ... that the only reason she can want to belong to the European Community is to oppose it.' Ironically it was her second husband-to-be that was running Thatcher's advertising campaign.

CHAPTER FIVE

Diamond days

By 1989 Nigella's love life had become characterized by her preference for the intellectual in need of mothering. She also seemed to have a thing for men in wigs. 'There was that scary lawyer, Geoffrey Robertson. He didn't need mothering at all,' remembered Sarah Johnson.

Nigella's father was unimpressed too, according to *Private Eye*: 'Her unsuitable consort is the media and civil rights barrister and left-wing firebrand whose battle honors include the *Oz* obscenity trial, the Michael X murder trial and the *Gay News* blasphemy trial.' Emily Lawson-Tancred, a lawyer herself, pleaded for the defense: 'Geoffrey Robertson was very hard working. He was an older man, an Australian lawyer working in John Mortimer's chambers. I think Nigella really enjoyed being around the kind of people working there – they were working in such interesting areas of law.'

The documentary film-maker Olivia Lichtenstein was there when they met. 'We were introduced by a mutual friend of hers who decided to set Nigella and me up (with

Geoffrey) at the same time. Understandably he chose Nigella.' Olivia, who went on to become one of Nigella's best friends ten years later, thought she was aloof and stand-offish at the time. 'She went out with said man for a couple of years,' she wrote in *Eve*, 'they broke up and I kept track of her over the years in a begrudging-of-her-success kind of way.'

Nigella was not happy when he left her for another literary star-in-the-making. 'I hear that Nigella Lawson, the Chancellor's daughter, is furious at the favorable reviews that have been given to a new novel by one Kathy Lette called *Girls' Night Out*,' teased *Private Eye*'s Grovel column. 'Literary editors have been made to feel that they have betrayed Nigella by allowing the book to be reviewed at all. For why? Nigella, who these days is beginning to look alarmingly like her father, was until recently the *inamorata* of gorgeous, pouting barrister Geoffrey Robertson QC. But then Robertson went on holiday Down Under and fell for an Australian writer; was so smitten with her, indeed, that he brought her back with him as a holiday souvenir and installed her in his house in place of Nigella. The woman in question, I need hardly add, is Kathy Lette.'

Twenty-nine-year-old Nigella ran to the arms of her big brother and confided in him about her disastrous love life and misguided penchant for intellectual barristers. Dominic, then editor of the *Spectator*, had read an article by a contributor from Nigella's workplace which had made him smile, and in an inspired moment planted a seed that would grow into one of the most successful media marriages of the twentieth century. Why, he suggested, didn't she go out with a nice boy like John Diamond? It was a *shiddach* (Yiddish for matchmaker) that would have made his mother *kvell* (swell with pride).

Nigella followed her brother's advice, and in 1989 she and Diamond began to share bagels at the *Sunday Times*. He had first noticed her 'like something from a metaphysical poem who smiled at me occasionally', wandering around the offices. She was still Deputy Literary Editor at this time, and he was the Deputy Travel Editor. He had been married already, and was with another girlfriend when he first met Nigella. It would be six months before their relationship would develop. 'I do remember lying on her bed one night watching TV and reaching across to kiss her and she said, "No, I don't think so." It was like Sophia Loren saying "no". Why would this woman possibly say "yes" to me?'

He was the only one of her boyfriends she was friends with first, and the only boyfriend who shared her Jewish roots. John's humor was what grabbed her attention first. One day he overheard her talking to a friend at work about whether or not she might be diabetic. She was busy describing her symptoms as being overweight and bad-tempered when John quipped, 'You're not diabetic, you're Jewish.'

An expenses-paid weekend for two was another attraction. John was in the enviable position of commissioning articles as Travel Editor on the paper and happened on a great idea for 'top ten getaways'. He gave Nigella Soho to explore, and saved Devon for himself. 'We had this weekend of doing things in London that Londoners never get to do, going to the theatre and the cinema,' he remembered. 'We slept in single beds and never laid a finger on each other.' The following weekend it was his turn to invite her to Devon. 'It was a weekend of sex,' said John.

John was good with his hands. He could fix things, especially dodgy computers, and had the kind of practical skills which other boyfriends never offered. 'He was also a very clever man,' remembered a boss of his at the *Sunday Times*. Nigella's friends were thrilled. 'John was so different from them all,' said Sarah. 'He came from an ordinary family, and he'd been round the houses. He was around normal people rather than the aristocratic nutters she used to hang out with. He was just an ambitious journalist with enough talent – not a huge amount, but enough – and used it the best way he could to earn a living. He was prepared to worship her and really looked after *her* for a change. I remember him writing in his column how it feels when someone who had just been voted forty-seventh most beautiful woman in the world or something pops her head around the door and asks him what he wants for lunch. He always said that the title for her book *How to be a Domestic Goddess* might have been ironic, but it wasn't to him. He was full of grace – in the religious sense. He felt truly blessed.'

One of John's colleagues on the *Sunday Times* said that John could never quite understand how he managed to persuade Nigella Lawson to fall in love with him. 'He could never get his head around the fact that this beautiful intellectual with such a pedigree was absolutely besotted with him. He always found it amazing. John has *chutzpah* in spades and he could write and he could talk and I think he probably laughed her into bed. He was very, very clever and he was great fun to be with. She must have liked him being so practical as well.'

Born in Stamford Hill in North London on 10 May 1953, John Diamond was the son of a biochemist (specializing in cancer research) and a fashion designer, and the youngest of three brothers. A scholarship at eleven had taken him to the City of London School, and at first it looked as though he would go into acting. Instead he trained as a drama teacher, and spent four years at Dalston Mount girls' school, where he met his first wife, Anne-Marie, a dance teacher working at a nearby school. John hated teaching, and, setting his sights on the media, snuck his way into the *Sunday Times* in time-honored fashion, after honing his skills with words on a local property paper and London's local listings magazine, *Time Out*. A quick flirtation with television landed him a job as a researcher on *The Six O'Clock Show*, and his charm, rather more than his talent, would win him jobs presenting shows as disparate as *Tomorrow's World*, *Stop Press*, *After Hours* and *Fourth Column*.

His culture was a heady mix of the media bars of Soho and the Hasidic capital of London, Stamford Hill. His family had come from Eastern Europe and then East London – Shadwell and Stepney, where his grandparents and parents were brought up, and Hackney and Stoke Newington, where he learned to kick a football and ride a bike. As the Jews moved north, leaving the Bengalis to take their turn to fill the streets of the East End with their food and clothing businesses, John wrote about this rich area of London in his column in *The Times*: 'A few years ago, I stayed in my brother's flat in the center of the area, surrounded by street signs, the names of which I'd first heard in stories of family mythology forty years earlier: Flower and Dean Walk, Tenter Ground, Old Montague Street. The kosher butchers were halal butchers now, the synagogues had had minarets added to them and become mosques, the broken-backed Jewish men who shuffled along Brick Lane had been transformed into broken-backed, shuffling Bengali men.'

He was comfortable in his Jewish skin, but didn't go to synagogue. 'I describe myself as a Jewish agnostic,' he wrote in one of his columns. 'I would say "atheist" but what would God think?' 'John Diamond was one generation away from the immigrants,' said Rabbi Dunner by way of explanation. 'Losing your sense of Jewishness is not so much about being upper class,' he added, comparing the Diamonds with the Lawsons. 'It's about how far you've worked your way into British society already.'

Somehow it's impossible to imagine Nigella sitting round the TV in the 1960s with her parents, reading out the list of Jewish names on the credits as all good Jews do, with the requisite sigh. For John, it was in his blood. 'I am turning into my late great-aunt Kenia', he wrote in the *Jewish Chronicle.* ' "Warren Mitchell," she'd say as the actors in *Till Death Us Do Part* were credited, and add meaningfully, "Warren *Meisel,* as was of course," or "Bernard Bresslaw; *Brady Boy,*" because as far as much of my family was concerned, every London Jew was branded for life by the East End youth club he or she had attended long decades earlier.' His family, he wrote, were obsessed with counting Jews. Aunt Fedya even claimed Bruce Forsyth as one of their own, prompting a row with Uncle Simmy. ' "Certainly," Fedya would say. "Forsyth? Ha! Finkel. You know the Finkels, used to run that bakery on Hessel Street?" And she'd give a look.'

His grandfather believed that his membership of a Board of Deputies sub-committee conferred on him the task of counting all the Jews in the world, and Friday nights, the weekly gathering of the clans, would begin with his grand-father opening the door and asking the boys to guess how many Jews there were in a particular country. 'We'd say we didn't know,' wrote John, faced with the task of guessing the number of Jews in Nepal one week. 'Go on. Guess. Five or 100,000?' 'Seventy-four,' replied his grandfather 'in an excited voice as though about to give us their names'. John had begun to do the same, perhaps not with the same vigor, and probably with more irony, when he began to notice that there were at least three Jews on the parish council in *The Vicar of Dibley*.

This was the beginning of a new decade in London, and yet being Jewish was still only cool in the pages of the *Jewish Chronicle*. Gloria Abramoff was the producer of BBC Radio's first Jewish program, which was broadcast on Greater London Radio (GLR). 'When we first set up "Jewish London" in 1990 it was absolutely impossible to get people on the program,' she said. 'I could never understand it. I was born off Bishop's Avenue in a ten-bed mansion and then my father lost his money and we lived in a one-bed flat in Golders Green, but I was always happy with my cultural roots. I always thought, "What's the big deal?"' It wasn't until 1995 when things began to change. 'It helped that we had Vanessa

[Feltz] because she was a serious presenter,' said Gloria. 'And then we got Wendy Robbins, who was a serious journalist, and they would ask proper questions. So then we did get Michael Grade, and Alan Yentob, David Baddiel and Sacha Baron Cohen. And it started. Suddenly people were prepared to come in and talk. The interest in genealogy meant that suddenly it was cool to be Jewish.'

One broadcaster making regular visits to GLR's arts shows, including 'Jewish London', was John Diamond. 'He was very interested in his Jewish culture,' said Christopher Silvester, who had become good friends with John, 'and much more than Nigella was. He used Yiddish expressions, and had that folklore at his disposal.' When there was an opening for a new presenter after Vanessa Feltz left to become queen of daytime TV, John was offered the job. Interestingly for the man who rarely said no, he declined, saying that he was too busy. Gloria was not sorry. 'He was really unattractive,' she said. 'I could never understand why he could be with a looker like Nigella. He only charmed people who would be of benefit to him and I don't think he realized I was the producer. He was cold, and he didn't seem to care that I was a Jewish woman. I didn't like him. I wasn't useful or pretty enough, and he made me feel very inadequate.'

One of his bosses on the *Sunday Times* agreed that he may well have treated people differently according to how well they might be able to serve his needs. 'I think John always knew who was useful to him. I was a superior in the hierarchy, although he was never sycophantic. I remember changing his copy and having quite a row about it. You didn't change John's copy without a row. He was quite brittle and harsh.'

Although John and Nigella were to become one of London's most popular media couples, they were surprisingly quiet about their relationship, even three years in. 'John Diamond was forced to reveal more than he would have liked about his domestic arrangements on last week's *Midweek* which he was presenting in Libby Purves's absence,' wrote *Private Eye* in 1992. 'Despite writing a column for *The Times* entitled "Private Life" every Thursday, he squirmed with embarrassment and then got quite ornery when one of the guests asked him to reveal who he lived with ... Diamond eventually gave in after an excruciating silence and confessed to living with someone called "Susan". Susan? He then went on to describe her as "shrewd Susan".'

John entertained London's network with his endless one-liners while Nigella looked like a goddess and cooked like a dream. Christopher Silvester remembers delightful evenings at Chesterton Road, just off Ladbroke Grove, on the outer edge of London's Notting Hill. 'It was a basement flat which had been decorated beautifully, and needless to say Nigella had a gorgeous kitchen installed, which had an Italian range with various fancy features, and she was very proud of that. The food was always excellent, but it wasn't done with any great effort. She loved making risottos. Lentils come to mind, but Puy lentils rather than the hippy-ish variety. And then I'm sure something like chocolate and orange mousse, something obviously fattening and delicious.'

This was before babies, when money was easy and opportunities were everywhere for them. They were becoming the people they had always wanted to be, making money writing about the things they loved most, often for the people they loved most. Many of them shared their holidays too. 'Nigella had found a villa in Porto Ercole, a couple of hours outside Rome. It belonged to the family of a British writer called Alan Moorhead, a very famous war correspondent who had written brilliant despatches in World War II,' said Christopher Silvester, who was one of those who accompanied the Lawson-Diamonds on holiday in the early nineties. 'I think she found it in the classified section at the back of the *Spectator.*' Nigella, still the restaurant critic for the *Spectator* at this time, led them on a forty-five-minute trek to find a restaurant she had heard about. 'It was in the basement of a farm building somewhere in the countryside of the Maremma region,' Silvester remembers. 'We had about seven courses, each of which was quite remarkable. That was a great meal, one of the best meals I have ever eaten, and it was Nigella who led us there that night.'

They were a party of ten, as Nigella wrote in her review of Lo Strambotto in the *Spectator*, including some Italian friends. The restaurant was, she wrote, a 'dream of the perfect Italian restaurant, a fantasy more often met by proxy in the writings of Elizabeth David and Jane Grigson'. Not that she informs her readers where to find it, other than it being somewhere near Porto Ercole. Ring, she advises, and they'll tell you. 'One turns up at some modest hostelry, is furnished with course upon course of delicious food, every ingredient, animal or vegetable, reared and grown in the next field, and with rough jugs of throaty yellow local wine just that morning squeezed from the vat by a cheerily aproned signora who at the end of lunch presses on you, as a modestly proud courtesy, a home-distilled aromatic and molten digestive, before handing you, some hours later, a bill for fourpence.'

Her friends were a sophisticated lot, but Nigella was already able to bring something extra to the table. 'She would talk it through, explaining why something was particularly to be savored. It was Nigella who introduced me to panna cotta puddings and prosecco sparkling wine. She was very keen on prosecco, I remember. We'd all be interested in what she had to say about food,' said Silvester.

Nigella was lyrical about the meal in her review: 'Rabbit was stuffed, studded with juniper berries, fennel seeds and needles of rosemary, rolled and cooked by that distinctively Italian method, both braised and roasted at the same time,' she wrote in the *Spectator*. 'The brasato had been cooked so slowly, so long, that the beef, thin, pale, wine-wet slices of it, was as sweet as carrot ... A plate of soft white goat's cheese came too, each small-cut square topped with gritty local honey. Only at the River Café in Hammersmith have I come across this combination before. It works. It's heaven.' Silvester and the rest of the group soaked up the anchovy butter and the poetry. 'She was unusual among my friends. Most people of my acquaintance didn't really talk about food that much. John was much the same. I was in my early thirties and although our food culture was changing we still didn't know very much about it.'

Imagine inviting someone who was discussing the merit of walnut oil when she was twenty, who would be a restaurant critic for twelve years, and was raised by generations of great cooks, to dinner. 'I once went to a dinner party a good friend of mine gave,' wrote Nigella in *How to Eat*, and somehow you just know it's not going to end well. 'She'd been up till three in the morning the night before making stocks. She said scarcely a word to any of us after opening the door, since she was in the middle of about five courses. The food was spectacular but she spent most of the evening ever more hysterical in the kitchen. At one point we could, as we stiltedly made conversation between ourselves, hear her crying.'

John and Nigella were glamorous in a Bohemian sense, their sitting room cluttered with books and people, and their kitchen piled with pots and utensils discovered in foreign flea markets. Nigella, once often spotted wearing a kaftan at book launches, was now allowing her inner goddess to play as she settled into her relationship with John, son of a fashion designer and grandson of a rag trader. Before John, Nigella had 'an extraordinary dress sense', according to Sarah Johnson. 'As a student she used to wear her father's pinstriped suits, which was a big mistake. You can't look like Katharine Hepburn when you look like Nigella; she looked more like Oliver Hardy. She also used to wear her hair in a snood for some reason. She used to go to Oxfam shops in Oxford and spend what little money she had on fifties dresses. She always used to say that she didn't have any money, and I think she really did think that. She was always very colourful in those fifties dresses.'

'Why are you wearing such baggy clothes and flat shoes?' John asked her when they became friends. 'And you should wear more make-up.' The feminist in Nigella was appalled and told him to 'go and find someone who wears Janet Reger underwear and a strappy dress'. But it wasn't long before she began to allow him to buy clothes for her. Nigella was experimenting with a more sophisticated fashion sense now, although she said that she had her own style before John started peeling off the layers and bringing out the glamour. 'I wasn't one of those who went to the office in miniskirts. He didn't remake my image,' she told Sue Lawley. She and her sister Thomasina were into fashion at an early age, although their look, in matching coordinates, was more backing singer than catwalk model. 'I'd be in miniskirt and flouncy shirt and Thomasina would be in trousers and a flouncy shirt,' she remembers.

By the time of their wedding party in 1992 she was wearing a strapless silk gown and a garland of ivy. John had made her feel secure enough to take off the mask and bring out the confidence, which is his legacy to her. 'You do well in life if you team up with someone who makes you feel good about yourself,' she told Sue Lawley.

They had tied the knot on a whim in Venice. The wedding itself was a secret, hurried affair appealing to Nigella's need to get married at a moment's notice: 'Thinking about it just makes me more aware of the pitfalls.' It may not have seemed to the outside world that she was scarred by her parents' divorce, but she would write in her column in 1995: 'The fear that children have of divorce seems entirely in pace with the probability of their being a victim of it. Thus it is a reasonable fear.'

If the wedding sounds like love's young dream, the reality wasn't quite as romantic. The ceremony was conducted in secret above the Department of Marine Pollution, and according to John 'it was such a rigmarole. We had to get special permission from the Foreign Office back in the UK and we decided that if things didn't come through we wouldn't bother. I can still see our assistant zooming up the Grand Canal on the morning of the wedding, waving the piece of paper that said "yes".'

John explained why they had decided to do something as proper as get married in an article he wrote for the *Daily Mail*. 'It does feel different being married. I find myself playing with my new ring with a grin on my face that is variously smug and wistful. I relish being described as my wife's husband rather than her partner, and she as my wife, even if I still have to think for a split second who's being referred to.' And in the week that the Office of Population Censuses and Surveys released the latest divorce figures (42 per cent in 1992) John was sure that it wouldn't happen to them. 'We all believe that we can buck the statistics,' wrote the fearless columnist. 'We drive cars, we smoke, we drink, we eat the wrong foods and we know that it is the other drivers, drinkers and smokers who will die in some intensive care unit or another. As far as I'm concerned, then let the other mad harriers live out their short and brutal married lives. Nigella and I will be the happy 58 per cent, supportive, loving, honest.'

Nigella told the *Telegraph*'s Nigel Farndale why she chose John. 'Often two people who are quite different get married, and you think you like someone because there is that difference. But actually – and this may sound like gobbledegook – what you are attracted to in the supposed difference is the chance it will give you to accept a part of yourself you didn't know you had, or you secretly knew you had but were embarrassed about. So for me that meant John's showy-offy character. Because I'm naturally shy. Over the years I probably took on a lot of that character. It turned me from being a quiet person to a constantly talking person. In the same way, he thought of himself as funny, and I was the serious one, and yet over the years he became more relaxed about not having to crack a joke every five minutes. In that sense, over time, you take on each other's characteristics and the differences evaporate.'

She said that she had changed since knowing him. 'I think I'm a quite useful brake on his exuberance in the same way that he makes me less cagey. I often think that in marriage, or with partners, you choose someone who expresses a side of you that for whatever reason you're not able to express yourself. I can talk through anything with John – it's part of the unspoken contract between us. Whatever I need to do or want from my life is thought of as every bit as important, if not more so, than John's. I'm happier for a variety of reasons, but inevitably if you like being with someone you end up with a less embattled view of life.'

If the wedding was a secret, private affair for Nigella, the wedding party when they got back to London was the grand affair that would have been John's fantasy. Nigella was the epitome of glamour, even hiring an expert make-up artist after doing her own in Venice. 'Because it wasn't a wedding,' she wrote in her column in *The Times* years later, 'I allowed myself an unbridal slick of red lipstick, but Derek is very good at understanding what a particular person as much as a particular face needs, so you can feel reassuringly relaxed in his hands. My brief to him was – and forgive my vain presumption – Rita Hayworth meets Snow White; I think he mastered his brief admirably.'

Christopher Silvester was John's best man. 'They took over the whole of the Groucho Club,' he said, referring to the Soho members' drinking club where they spent much of the late eighties and early nineties watching the doors swing open every couple of minutes to announce the arrival of another media starlet and newspaper editor. Dominic took on the traditional role of father of the bride, giving Nigella away to her new husband, while Nigel Lawson looked on from the crowd. 'I don't think that his wife was there,' Silvester said of her father.

It was a guest list that would have thrilled John's aspirant soul. The brand-new BBC Director General, John Birt, then controller of BBC1 Alan Yentob, novelists Douglas Adams and Martin Amis, editor of the *Sunday Times* Andrew Neil, restaurant PR Elizabeth Crompton-Batt and her husband Alan, who was known as the founder of modern PR, and editor of *Vogue*, Alexandra Shulman were among the hundreds of what John and his parents would have called serious *ganza mucha*. It was the place to be seen, with some people even risking their neck to be there. *Private Eye*'s Grovel took the opportunity to thumb his social columnist's nose at the *Daily Mail*. 'My old friend, Nigel Dempster, has set himself up as the expert on the whereabouts of Islamically challenged author Salman Rushdie. Had he been present at the wedding party for John Diamond and Nigella Lawson at the Groucho Club recently, Pratt-Dumpster would no doubt have been surprised to catch sight of Rushdie – since a few days before he had claimed that Rushdie had emigrated to Finland.'

John was among the prolific young journalists for whom life was a natural networking exercise, packed with plenty of John's tipple, Paddy whiskey, champagne and expense account lunches. Michael VerMeulen, then editor of *GQ*, who would die of a cocaine overdose in 1995, Paul Spike, a food critic for Vogue, his on-off girlfriend and soon to be wife Alexandra Shulman, the magazine's editor, 'bad boy' journalist Toby Young and a flock of others joined John at the bar, shared contacts and stories and argued about everything. 'We were a collection of mavericks,' Christopher Silvester recalled. 'We inhabited the same world. He joined the *Mirror* while I was writing about Robert Maxwell for *Private Eye*. I got to know his editor, Roy Greenslade, very well. He and his wife, the journalist Noreen Taylor, became very close friends with both John and Nigella. John even bought a plot of land on Lough Swilly, in County Donegal, Ireland, near to where Roy and Noreen had bought a Georgian manor house. He and Nigella had gone over to stay with Roy and Noreen and they had fallen for the area. He eventually wanted to build a small house there. He was doing a radio show about the press for the BBC and I appeared on it a couple of times as a guest. We were all seeing each other for drinks and doing much the same things as each other.' It was a perfect balance of work and play.

Among Silvester's finest moments were his occasional jazz evenings at the Groucho, where his friends and other members would pack into the brasserie at the back for dinner while Christopher – grandson of the band leader Victor Silvester – crooned jazz songs, often supported by his uncle-by-marriage, Barry Martin, a Jewish actor. 'John and Nigella would come along to my gigs and I remember John enjoyed chatting to my uncle about show business and Jewish folk-lore. Also, he was always threatening to bring along his saxophone to accompany me.'

'They used to have this wonderful summer solstice party at their home in Goldhawk Road,' Silvester remembered. ('Moving west was "a condition of betrothal",' wrote John in his column in *The Times* by way of explanation of how a nice Jewish boy ends up outside the self-styled ghetto of North London.) According to Silvester, theirs 'was a very comfort-able, West London semi-detached house, with a long garden at the back, and they would have this very grand catered party for all their friends and journalistic contacts. John and Nigella were great networkers. John was very sociable and loved being well-known, but he couldn't have been more pleased when Nigella became famous. When they enter-tained, the thing you noticed was that everyone who was there sort of belonged. Of course, we were always seeking patronage and job offers. But people were there because they wanted to be, because they liked being with John and Nigella. John in particular really gloried in the names they could attract, but I never felt there was anything cheap or dishonest about it. There was a streak of good, old-fashioned vulgarity about him which he would readily mock himself for. John's family would be there and there would be loads of TV people, literary people, food people, and people who were in John's gambling circle.'

John was the classic aspirant Jew, and was skipping along a meteoric path to power, playing poker and Scrabble with the big boys such as Charles Saatchi, Alan Yentob and Michael Green. 'He loved hobnobbing with well-off and successful Jews,' laughed Silvester. 'It didn't matter whether they had inherited their wealth or whether they'd made it. But there was also that down-to-earth aspect of him which never lost touch with the friends that he'd made when he was younger.'

Their world was full of friends who were beginning to rise to prominence or had already got there, and who would set much of the media agenda. Carlton Television's Charles Elton, then an independent TV producer, and his journalist wife Lucy Heller (sister of novelist Zoe, whose book *Notes on a Scandal* is due to become a major film starring Judi Dench and Cate Blanchet) were close to the couple. Award-winning war correspondent Janine di Giovanni, Nigella's old Oxford friend and now an executive producer at BBC Films, Tracey Schofield and her husband, the novelist and director Hanif Kureishi, were regular dinner guests. Nick Howard, whose family owns Castle Howard and whose father was Director General of the BBC, and his wife Vicky Barnsley, who owned Fourth Estate Publishing and who now runs HarperCollins, were just some of the people who would pop over for a bowl of pasta.

Sarah Johnson said that her social life wasn't always so glamorous. 'When we moved into Shepherd's Bush in the mid-nineties I had two small children and a babe in arms and Nigella rang and said, "Right, I'm off to Waitrose. What can I get for you?" I should be a lot more jealous of her because she's so beautiful and successful, but I'm not. She's been such a loyal friend.'

CHAPTER SIX

Thomasina's legacy

Thomasina and Nigella, with only sixteen months between them, were exceptionally close. Sarah Johnson said that Thomasina was a 'typical Lawson to look at, with gorgeous dark brown eyes. She was the solid sister, the good one who did sensible things. Nigella was very proud that she was an occupational therapist, that she did good things for people.'

'We cooked a lot together,' Nigella told Justine Picardie, whose sister Ruth also died of breast cancer, 'and when she was living in Wales and I was in London we had endless conversations about what we were eating for our respective dinners. We always had rituals about food; *How to Eat* is full of recipes for her, my favourite family ones.'

In 1994 Nigella was living with Emily Lawson-Tancred in London's Queen's Park while Thomasina became ill, although she had moved in with John by the time she died. 'She was ill for a long time,' said Emily. 'I can't remember how long, but she went through radiotherapy and it was all very difficult. She was a lovely girl, a very smiley person. She and Nigella were terribly close.' 'When Thomasina was dying, I pleaded with God,' Nigella told a journalist later. 'I said, "If she gets better, I'll be the most religious person in the world," and a fat lot of good that did me.' 'She was my other half,' she told journalist Andrew Duncan. 'We did everything together. I thought I'd never recover from her death. It was like part of me being taken away, but I find I developed some of her toughness. She was really the "older" sister.'

Nigella was nine months pregnant with Cosima when Thomasina died, and almost as soon as the funeral was over, she went into labor. She laughed when people suggested that perhaps there was some kind of compensation in the birth of her daughter. 'But you can't think, well, my sister's dead but, hey, this will make it better,' she told Sally Vincent in the *Guardian*. 'And when people said at New Year, here's hoping you have a better year, you think, why, is she coming back? There is a kind of euphoria of grief, a degree of madness,' she said. 'You are very distanced from other people because what is going on in your head is literally unshareable and you can't focus properly on what is going on outside you. And, in a funny way, each death is different and you mourn each death differently and each death brings back the death you mourned earlier and you get into a bit of a pile-up.'

When she talks about the deaths and the dying in her family, she's as stiff-upper-lipped as the next British toff. But at the mention of Thomasina she buckles: 'I did get a bit hysterical the night Thomasina died, actually,' she told Andrew Billen in the *Evening Standard*. 'When I got back, the next night I mean, it was just a kind of nightmare. I was completely ... ' and the Nigella Lawson who is always in control, always able to express just why she doesn't cry, is finally speechless.

'Nigella was very private about how she felt about the deaths of her mother and her sister,' Emily said. 'But I think she was quite devastated. When her mother died, her grandmother sent us both to Corsica on holiday afterwards. I didn't have any money – I was a student at the time. Nigella didn't really want to talk about how she felt. You could feel it, though, in the silence. I think when something so awful like that happens to you there's an empty, silent feeling in you and you can't talk about it because it's just that – empty and silent. You feel quite separate from the world. If you talk about it somehow you're making it into a drama. I remember a friend making a comment to her about how she appeared not to mind about Thomasina's death, and she was appalled and asked her, "How can you possibly know how I'm feeling?" She was with John when Thomasina died so she would have talked to him about anything that she wanted to. She wouldn't have needed to talk to her friends too.'

Bruce Goodison, the director who was responsible for her early TV image, said that she and her sister Horatia often use their disarming sense of humor to deal with their tragedies. 'The thing about them is that they're both stiff-upper-lipped about emotions but will then confuse you by making a funny comment about death. They'll say something that seems really inappropriate like, "You can't have the highs without the deaths." I've just made a film about people who have lost people tragically and they will say things in a jovial way that are devastating for the person listening. You just don't know how to respond.'

Nigella, an Oxford undergraduate, at the Piers Gaveston Ball at The Park Lane Hotel, London, May 1983.

Nigel Lawson, then Chancellor of the Exchequer, plays French cricket with Emily (3), Tom (5) and his second wife, Therese, at their constituency home of Stoney Stanton, Leicestershire, March 1985.

Nigel and Therese pose outside No. 11 Downing Street before the Budget of March 1985, the year that Nigella's mother died of cancer.

The Chancellor of the Exchequer, Nigel Lawson, with his second wife, Therese, and their children, Tom (10) and Emily (5), March 1987.

Nigella at Sarah Johnson's wedding at the Traveller's Club in Pall Mall, April 1988. Nigella kept this picture on her desk at the *Sunday Times*.

Nigella (29), the literary pundit, attends the Booker Prize dinner, 1989.

to me and the baby utterly oblivious to her stirrings or crying, or on the sofa or in his study.'

By October 1995 Nigella was away for a weekend without the baby, and it was John's turn to look after Cosima. By the end of the Saturday he had a plan. 'I phoned the nanny and gave her time-and-a-half to come in on a Sunday,' he wrote. This wasn't his first time in sole charge, of course; only a couple of weeks earlier he had taken her out for an afternoon at the bookmakers; 'Cosima watched it with me on the TV set in the shop, she going "Horsey! Horsey!" And the rest of the clientele, hardly more intelligibly, screaming the name of the horse she'd picked. The horse came third from last.'

Christopher Silvester thinks that John underplayed his paternal abilities in his column. 'I remember John taking me into another room to change Cosima's nappy one evening while Nigella was preparing dinner. He was very proud of his ability to change nappies. He had these big hands, hands that you might think were better suited to dismantling the engine of his Harley-Davidson, yet he was very gentle and proceeded with great delicacy. He asked me to feel the downy skin on the back of Cosima's neck, and I remember him saying that he'd never felt anything softer than that tiny patch of skin. He was besotted with the experience of being a father.'

By the time Nigella and John had a small child running their life, it had turned into a liberal version of *Upstairs Downstairs* with a gardener, a cleaner and a procession of nannies. 'It's only a matter of time,' wrote John, 'before we have a bloke in striped trousers at the front door asking who should he say is calling.' But although they were embarrassed, as socialists always are when they outsource their responsibilities to the low paid and underqualified, they got over it quickly enough and hired 'Tatyana' (not her real name) whom John described in his column as 'a giantess of a New Zealander'. After coming over as 'a real person' at her interview, they soon discovered that she had 'a habit of upending the fridge and tipping the contents down her throat' and telling Cosima, then two, that the monsters who lived in the garden would eat her unless she sat quietly while *The Lion King* was on. She was promptly given her marching orders and sent back to the agency to be palmed off on another unsuspecting family.

The Amazonian nanny pretty soon landed on another family. When a nanny is placed by an agency, the prospective family tends to check her out directly with the previous employers, and when my source found out that they were the Lawson-Diamonds his wife rang up for a reference. 'Nigella told her that Tatyana had only just joined her family but that while she couldn't recommend her too highly she wasn't gregarious or talkative enough to fit into her scheme of things as she and John Diamond and her children loved nannies that engaged more with them as a family. We said fine and were happy to get someone at such short notice.'

It was only then that they found out that the monster in the garden was Tatyana herself. 'Within a few days Tatyana emerged as a walking disaster. She was so incompetent she ended up locking our youngest child inside the house with her and the older child still outside and no one else inside. In the end she had to get the Fire Brigade to break into the house, where our child had had the sense to go into his bedroom and was found peacefully asleep in his bed.'

Amazonian nannies don't get to be six foot on a diet of Ryvita either. 'We were giving a dinner party,' he remembered. 'The food had been prepared and was sitting in the kitchen while we ate through earlier courses in the adjacent dining room. Tatyana bounded back from the gym, gave a friendly wave to us and then proceeded to devour one of the main courses sitting on the side. It later transpired that this was the cause of her downfall in the Lawson household. We were told by a mutual friend that Nigella had painstakingly prepared various dishes for a *Vogue* shoot and had left them all cling-filmed up in her refrigerator awaiting the photographer. Tatyana sauntered in, saw these exciting-looking dishes and picked her way through them all, leaving a tangle of bones and other detritus on the dainty plates. Following Nigella's lead, we also dumped her within a couple of weeks. Tatyana was so dumb she actually later asked her next prospective employers to get a reference from us, which we gave as honestly as we could.'

In fairness, John did put his hands up about this in his column. 'You phone up the agency and tell them that actually things aren't working out, no, absolutely nothing major, just a personality clash sort of thing and Tatyana disappears for a couple of afternoons to see if other couples can spot her psychopathy, and eventually a couple phones to say, "We've just interviewed Tatyana and she seems super. How have you found her?" to which you want to answer "Well, we just looked in the larder and there she was with her mouth round a family-sized packet of digestives and the bread knife in her hand." But you can't.'

Nannies bring out the best and the worst in parents; for working parents they can be a lifeline. When one of her nannies announced to Nigella that she wanted to leave to pursue a degree, Nigella responded as if her life depended on her – largely because it did. 'Nigella has always been sweet and extremely fair to people who work with her as well as for her,' said one of her previous employees. 'But she does react to stress. She's an incredibly able woman, but with two small children and a husband who was dying for a long time, she really needed people not to let her down.'

'I'm not a TV presenter kind of mum,' Nigella told Sue Lawley, 'but I do cuddles.' 'I'm very bad at looking after children in a proper way,' she told Justine Picardie, 'but making cupcakes is something that we do together – we have a big bowl of mixture and I do minimalist cakes while they sprinkle every possible decoration on top of theirs, with icing that's three times the weight of the cake.' But, she said, she doesn't have a sweet tooth. 'I can have a house full of chocolate but I'd rather eat bread and cheese. It's the act of baking that I find calming, and there's something very pleasurable in providing a cake for a friend.'

The kids have grown up trying her afternoon experiments and are 'adventurous eaters'. They have their limits, Nigella admits: Bruno will eat squid, which Cosima won't touch, and she can barely keep up with their changing taste buds. 'They love something one week and think it's disgusting the next week,' she said. 'Left to their own planning, my children would want pasta with butter every day. The other day I gave them minestrone. My son tried to be nice. He said, "It may look disgusting, but it tastes good." I love that kids are so honest about food. Adults worry about a status thing and don't want to be liking this or that if it's not in style, whereas children don't make those kinds of distinctions. They like both chicken nuggets and steamed mussels. Why should one food be good and the other bad?'

Sarah Johnson and Emily Lawson-Tancred have more adult-focused relationships with Nigella, although Sarah said that Nigella does have a profoundly motherly streak. 'I don't see her with her children, although they were running around at the launch of *Feast*. I would be unbelievably surprised if anyone were to say that she wasn't an excellent mother.'

By the mid-1990s Nigella was the columnist *de nos jours*, writing for the *Spectator*, the *Evening Standard*, the *Guardian* and the *Observer* as well as the *Daily Telegraph* and *The Times*. And it wasn't long before her food column in *Vogue* magazine would attract the attention of publishers Random House. Emily Lawson-Tancred watched her old flat-mate blossom. 'John helped with the packaging of her. She continued with what she was doing and who she was, but I think he helped to build her confidence. He encouraged her greatly. They were both freelancers living together, and having him around all the time after being alone in her flat getting on with her work made her much more confident.' Christopher Silvester suggested that it wasn't just John that was helping her mature as a writer: 'I don't think that he was the only influence. She wasn't a tabula rasa. She had her intellectual gifts and she'd had other experiences before John.'

Journalists usually concentrate on a main area of interest, and despite having full lives and a suitably wide range of interests they are often squeezed into a box marked 'Food' or 'Sport'. Someone interested in books surely can't be into make-up. How can a make-up expert know anything about food? But Nigella's is a life of many privileges, and one of those privileges was to be given columns of her own on topics of her choice. Columns are the hot air of newspapers and magazines, occasionally witty enough to be memorable, but generally little more than an opportunity for editors to mark off another space on the flat plan. The *Daily Mail*'s Peter McKay agrees, although he added that they are 'the furniture in a newspaper. You have to have them otherwise it's all news and features.' Certainly John and Nigella's columns in the early days were little more than an exercise in stretching their literary wings, and both of them wrote about whatever thought popped into their heads over the washing up.

Private Eye's Hackwatch column detailed the endless articles devoted to the couple's spats as a riposte to Nigella's earlier proclamation: 'The columnist as self-publicist is not an attractive spectacle.' 'Washing up last night,' Nigella wrote in August 1995, 'I found I could not put the stuff away afterwards. This wasn't laziness, as all male readers will recognize, but a desire to make apparent the labor I'd undertaken. This is normal behaviour for men, who expect to be applauded for domestic undertakings.'

'I hesitate to bother you with the drearily intimate details of my domestic life,' John wrote in October 1995. Hackwatch gave a synopsis of John's current moan: 'He is furious to discover that Nigella has washed his jeans without removing several checks from the pockets. Still, the anger eventually subsides and domestic bliss is restored. Or is it? On the same day, *The Times* Weekend section carries a two-page cover story by Nigella Lawson on the uselessness of the modern father, and in particular of J. Diamond.'

Nigella's columns were by this time almost always to do with shopping, make-up or food. There was the occasional outrage at the media coverage of Rwanda, the Queen's slipped vowels or the unfair dismissal of a pregnant army officer, but for the most part she was eloquently fluffy: 'Of course I'm not saying that spending £293,000 on flowers in 20 months is indicative of restraint or budget-conscious housekeeping,' she wrote in the *Observer* about Elton John's excesses. 'But, truly, if you were as rich as Elton John, would you feel the need for either? Far from seeing anything to sneer at in his response to the question, "£293,000 on flowers alone; is that possible?" – the disarming, "Yes, I like flowers" – I find it positively engaging.'

She even launched a scathing attack on the favorite pastime of half the population in her column in *The Times*. Suggesting that British newspapers devoted a 'ludicrous' amount of coverage to sport compared to the number of column inches they should be giving to 'Bosnia and children', she had male commentators in a state of apoplexy. 'In a demented article,' said Ian Wooldridge in the *Daily Mail*, 'Nigella Lawson, daughter of our Chancellor, went bananas over the amount of space British newspapers devote to sport.'

But, best of all, she loved to write about food, food obsessions, eating, restaurants, diets and eating disorders –

anything that food itself inspired. She could pull a column out of a conversation she'd had with a friend as easily as she could make a last-minute supper for ten out of a box of Arborio and some parmesan. An expanding waistline was as chaotic as a messy house, she inferred in her column for *The Times* in 1997, obviously after spending the morning staring at the state of her bedroom. 'It's about control, or lack of it,' she wrote. 'However disparagingly we might speak about those rigorously disciplined people who exercise absolute control on themselves and their environment, we tend to admire them, in admittedly an envious fashion. Fat, on the other hand,' she continues in her bid to convince herself that a tidy house is a tidy size 10, 'inspires such loathing, out of proportion to any mere aesthetic dismay ... it smacks of lack of restraint, of dreaded incontinence. We have more sympathy with anorexics than we do for compulsive eaters. Someone whose mental disorder shows itself in not eating at least gets thin. Someone whose unhappiness makes them eat too much just gets fat and that is where we lose sympathy. We're too appalled to be concerned.'

Later she would come to refer to diet as a four-letter word, with no place in polite society. 'If you want to diet,' she said in her column in the *Evening Standard* in January 1999, 'then you have to take the responsibility yourself, not draft everyone else into the diet police. It's bad enough you need to lose weight, but drawing people's attention to it is intoler-able. I can't bear references to weight loss either, but every time someone said, "You've lost weight" I hear "You were fat".'

Nigella may love her food, but she'll never allow herself to get fat again. 'I've put on so much weight,' she moaned when she was filming the second series of *Nigella Bites* in 2002. 'I don't want to be thin, but I'm better when I'm not putting on weight. That's one reason women are prone to be on my side, but I'm also quite a girls' girl.' The journalist from *Delicious* magazine looked sceptical. 'Those oft-remarked-upon, vulnerable, soft brown eyes, alabaster skin, the satisfying plumpness, recipe tastings dripping with sexual allure,' he wrote. 'I'm a boys' girl too,' she added, smiling.

The teenager who wore tents and glasses and her father's pinstriped suit, and the twenty-something whom John Diamond helped to prise out of baggy clothes and flat shoes, are no more. 'I have to admit that I felt awful when I put on weight after the birth of my first child and better when I lost it.' She's done Atkins, and left it behind in favor of a generally low-carb feast, and is now getting into yoga. She said she does keep an eye on the calories, but her ability to count them is like her cooking – more instinctive than scientific. 'I zero-rate Marmite, Bovril, soy sauce, Vietnamese and Thai fish sauce, all herbs, cabbage, carrot, onions, mushrooms, courgettes, mangetouts and sugar-snap peas, green or French beans, spinach, chard, pak choi, and all that leafy stuff, all lettuces, baby sweetcorn, baby asparagus, turnips, leeks and pretty well any vegetable that isn't starchy. There's no easy way to lose weight, but that's what works for me.'

According to Nigella, dinner for the weight-conscious foodie should be Thai or Japanese (although she omits to mention that coconut milk in Thai cooking is high in fat). 'They draw on intense flavors and fill you without supplying much fat,' she wrote. 'Italian food is also robustly flavored but it uses much more oil. It is healthy but you will put on more weight.' Balance rather than extremes is the key, she said, and in a fabulously two-fingered salute to the diet industry her tip for weight loss includes an individual pre-packed portion of steak and kidney pudding from M&S.

Being around food for the filming meant that she tended to eat less of it. Cooks everywhere will tell you that by the time they've tested the sauce, chewed a bit of the pasta to check its consistency or checked the meat for seasoning, they're less likely to pile the finished result on their own plate. Buffets at her launches are more difficult for her. 'The refugee mentality comes out in me,' Nigella said. 'I act as though I'll never have another meal.'

On a more ordinary kind of day her intake is as elegant and trashy, bloodthirsty and upper crust as you'd imagine. She told Andrew Harrison in *Word* magazine in 2003 what you might expect *chez* Lawson on an average day: 'Two boiled eggs. Four minutes. And they're special Italian eggs from a Greek grocer in Notting Hill. They've got a richer, more eggy flavor, and a fabulous colour. I use them all the time now. I'm not particularly precious about food – sometimes I do a toasted sandwich for the children with a little square of plastic ham and plastic cheese, and it is delicious – but I have become more squeamish. Usually if I miss a meal I start to get murderous and suicidal, but we had some ham on a shoot yesterday that was the slimy, injected stuff that must be the gleanings from the abattoir floor somewhere ... I just couldn't do it. I don't mind any form of innards – I can eat anything, and I love brains. I don't even know if you can still get them.' This is the girl who as a child called blood 'red gravy'. She draws the line only at 'bleached chickens' bottoms'.

After years of idle chit-chat in her columns, it was in *Vogue*'s food page that she found her true voice. It ran from Christmas 1995 to April 2001, with a brief return visit in January 2002, although with no mention of the gap after John died in March 2001, and was to really secure her foothold on the culinary stage. Here she could spread her wings and remember the food of her childhood and her mother's tips. Her mother, she told us in her first column, 'soaked a J cloth in melted butter and cooked the turkey with this fat yielding bandage strapped to its breast in an effort to prevent that stringy dryness that most people assume characterises turkey flesh.' It was the kind of evocative and nostalgic writing that would characterise her bestselling books over the years.

Here she could indulge a growing habit of food books and kitchen equipment. She told us where she shops, an act of generosity she continued in her books. She encouraged her readers to buy the best, and, where possible, local produce. She did not, however, always explain the practicalities, as a *Daily Mail* reader who followed her advice in *Nigella Bites* found to her cost. Miss Ross, an IT consultant from Wembley, rang Denise Bell at Heritage Prime, an organic meat supplier in Bridport, Dorset who told her that the cost would be £10.90 per kilo. It seems Ross did not realise that buying pork from a farmer was not the same as buying from a butcher. 'I gave her my credit card details as I just thought I was buying some pork' said Ross. 'She then said it would cost £416 before putting the phone down. I realised I'd just paid £400 for a bit of pig.'

'What the book does not reveal', said *The Mail*, 'is that the minimum pork order from Heritage Prime is a quarter pig.

With the other ingredients and wine, Miss Ross worked out her dinner for six was going to cost £450.' Not realising that she had actually bought enough meat to fill her freezer, she phoned the company back to cancel but was unable to get hold of anyone until the payment had been put through and the company said it was too late to cancel. Denise Bell said in defence of the local producer, that the price of her pigs reflects the time and dedication it takes to produce this quality of meat. She told me that Miss Ross who called at 8pm might not have realised that in order to fulfil her order, she would have had to be up at 5am to butcher said pig and courier it in time for Miss Ross' dinner party.

At *Vogue*, Nigella practiced the art of mentoring without patronising, even if sometimes the balance wasn't quite right. 'You don't need to make yourself suffer,' she told us in her first column, 'staggering back exhausted and resentful with ten days' food ... Most branches of Marks and Spencer will be open on Christmas Eve and again on Wednesday 27th, and the same goes for Waitrose and Sainsbury's ...' She added helpfully for those who don't get to the High Street much, 'And if you really are in need of intensive retail therapy, the Fifth Floor at Harvey Nichols – also hardly closing – has set up a Festive Food Service to help with Christmas-related food moans, worries and associated traumas.'

By 1998 she had made her class act into an art form. 'Now I don't know why I haven't told you this before,' she wrote, 'it's so obvious; the thing missing from most of your lives is a pressure cooker. I am not being cute; this is no retro pose. It's true, the idea of pressure cookers belongs to a gloriously naff surburban past, along with the hostess trolley and the fondue set.' And Nigella was set on a path to become the nation's Jiminy Cricket, nudging, reinventing and becoming an icon for an upper-crust generation of foodies. More than a mentor, she was a style leader, trashing the formal dinner party and introducing the idea of having friends round for dinner. Cooking, she pronounced, was about not going to too much effort but still managing to look good.

She was on a mission to bring out the domestic gods and goddesses in us all. While she was writing *How to Eat*, *Vogue* spotted an opportunity to claim the UK's latest book cook as their own, and hinted at what she would become as early as May 1998: 'Superwoman and Supermarkets: Nigella Lawson on the art of making the big shops work for you,' proclaimed her column headline. It even allowed her to experiment with the title 'Domestic Goddess' as early as 1998, as well as dive into the culinary cultures she would later plunder to fill her books.

The International issue of *Vogue* in September 1998 allowed her to look at American food in a way that most of us never had before. Ploughing through books such as Robert Clark's biography of the 'great American gastronome', James Beard, she began to carve out a career that took shape over the next five years, deepening her understanding of the greatest market of them all. 'We might think that groovy British eclecticism is the fount and origin of our current culinary celebrity, but we'd be wrong,' she enthused. 'Contemporary food, like the contemporary culture from which it springs, is American. The now scorned Nouvelle Cuisine, which earlier whetted our appetite for gastro excitement, was nominally French, but it was, more accurately, its

Californian incarnation that took root over here, while the neo-Mediterranean taste for culinary rusticana that has since taken over is really a roughed-up form of Manhattan Italian. We have therefore been liberated by our lack of classicism and that in itself is a very American quality.'

It seems that publishers love to leaf through the surreal world of designer lifestyle, high art and celebrity voyeurism, and in the autumn of 1998 *Vogue* columnists were weighing down the shelves with their food books. UK *Vogue*'s Arabella Boxer updated her book *The New First Slice Your Cookbook* with Grub Street, US *Vogue* food critic Jeffrey Steingarten published *The Man Who Ate Everything* through Headline, and Australian *Vogue*'s food editor Joan Campbell brought out *Bloody Delicious: A Life with Food* through Allen & Unwin in the UK. And Chatto & Windus published a work by Nigella Lawson which was deemed seminal in the UK, and which would change the eating habits of a generation. It was called *How to Eat*.

CHAPTER SEVEN

How to Eat

John's illness began with a simple but malignant lump in his neck in 1997, and although it was dismissed at first, it soon became clear that things were not going to be OK. Had the first tests in another hospital three months earlier not been wrong, and had he had the lump taken out earlier, maybe things would have been different. 'You can't go on thinking like that,' said Nigella, ever the pragmatist.

By 1998 he had had a major operation to remove his epiglottis and what remained of his tongue, his oesophagus had been moved, he'd had a tracheotomy to help his breathing and his food had to be consumed through a tube directly into his stomach. The loss of his voice was heartbreaking, not just for the family and friends, but for his Radio 4 fans; John was not just an award-winning and prolific writer, a Columnist of the Year in 1997 for the *What the Papers Say* Awards and shortlisted for the 1999 Samuel Johnson Prize. He was also a broadcaster, presenting *Fourth Column* and *After Hours* for BBC Radio, as well as appearing on TV shows. 'John felt that his voice was a large part of who he was,' Nigella said as she unveiled a plaque at the Royal Marsden Hospital after his death in 2001 to mark the opening of a state-of-the art voice laboratory in his memory. 'Being unable to speak as a result of the cancer and necessary treatment was understandably a huge loss.'

Covering the hole in his throat with elegant polo necks and tipping champagne directly into his tube were the kind of flourishes that showed just what he thought of the Grim Reaper. Asking to see the removed tumor, to actually touch his enemy, set the tone for how he was going to treat this disease. The tumor was a dark, hard lump with a white, oily center. 'It looks like an octopus,' said Nigella. 'Squid,' corrected the surgeon. It was the result of years of smoking. This John pointed out to a Mrs W of Virginia Water who had written to ask him for advice on how to stop her sons' new habits. 'I smoked from the age of thirteen until some time in my mid-thirties when, a veteran two-pack-a-day man, I swapped the fags from some nicotine gum, cigars and cigarettes,' he wrote, directing his answer to her sons. 'You have probably never met someone with this illness; I hadn't either. More to the point, you have met thousands of people with a fag in their hand who look healthy enough, who talk without dribbling and eat a meal without coughing it all over the tablecloth and don't fix you with a rheumy eye and tell you about the number of tubes an eight-hour operation causes to be poked into you. I am the walking, talking – or maybe not talking – equivalent of all those schoolday films of blackened lungs and tar-filled test-tubes, the films that never stopped me smoking because the films were about smoking in a different universe.'

Not that he wanted to leave a legacy, but possibly because he wanted to show this disease for what it really was, he wrote in his book *C: Because Cowards Get Cancer Too*, 'By all means campaign for some phantom "right" to smoke, but don't believe that right derives from corrupting the statistics about what smoking does to you. Understand it for what it is: the right to play Russian roulette, as I did, with the immune system.'

Not only could he no longer speak properly (he compared his voice to 'Charles Laughton in an underwater version of *The Hunchback of Notre Dame*') but he couldn't eat Nigella's food – or indeed anyone else's – despite the irony that he had never much liked the stuff in the first place. 'He's an old-fashioned meat and potatoes man, and he likes bought things like steak pies,' Nigella told *Waitrose* magazine. 'When I've made a pizza, my daughter Cosima always said, "Why can't I have one in a box like Daddy?" John always ate the Hawaiian sort with chunks of pineapple. What I miss is no longer being able to buy some vile thing to show him how much I love him. It took years to get him to eat a chickpea. Sometimes he just comes into the kitchen to smell what's cooking. I have girl-friends round and people come to Saturday and Sunday lunch. When his speech improves, I hope he'll be able to cope with being there at dinner. At the moment, it makes people uncomfortable.'

Her friend and BBC producer Olivia Lichtenstein suggested making a film for BBC's *Inside Story* called *Tongue Tied*, charting John's journey through the illness. Nigella was appalled when John told her. She told him that on no account would she agree. It was too late. He had already said yes. 'When he said he'd agreed to do a television film without consulting me I was horrified and upset. I'm glad we did, though. It's a wonderful film.'

The documentary took up the story in June 1997 with John's diagnosis. His speech was still intact and he talked about the disease as a writer would, researching it for a character he was developing, trying on the pain, feeling his way around the prospect of not being here any more. The camera followed him for the next two years as he went under the surgeon's knife again and again until his voice was utterly unrecognizable, and his initial chirpy distance from his illness was reduced to a much more poignant realism. 'Fancy having an operation which means that you can't kiss your children for a couple of months,' actor Michael Bywater read from his column in the documentary, 'and not having a voice to tell them why.'

Nigella was astonishingly stoical in the film, by his side physically and emotionally at all times, and leader of the intimate team of people – including his speech therapist and children Cosima and Bruno – who by 1999 were the only ones who could understand what he was saying. Always in control, she was human but dry-eyed, getting on with life with the kids, and working on her first commission from Chatto & Windus, while John learned how to use a syringe for his liquid food, how to live without a tongue and how to eat.

It is a bizarre and painful film to watch – and was equally so when first screened in 1999. How anyone could let the camera into such a traumatic experience is extraordinary, but Nigella was big enough to indulge him. As he hummed for the camera while filling his feeding syringe, as he strummed his guitar and sang to a dodgy 12-bar blues rhythm, 'Woke up this morning. Got cancer,' adding 'I'm working on the second verse,' as he jokily winced when the nurse attached his wristband to one of the few places on his body that didn't hurt, he was playing to the camera. But somehow you know that he'd have put on the same performance if it was for a friend visiting the house, that his way of dealing with the unimaginable would be to make a joke in public and to sink to terrible lows in private. Even the poignancy of the way he described his feelings about not being able to watch the children grow up is articulate and inevitably jerked the viewers' tears.

Of course it's real, but this is a man who refused to surrender his role as narrator of his own life. 'John is very open,' Nigella told the camera. 'My way of coping is distancing myself. If I was connecting with the words, it would be unbearable.' Some media watchers were more cynical. One said that his deathbed was offered to the media as a death scene. 'Dominic rang up a leading journalist who was a friend of all of them to say that if he wanted to pay a visit to Diamond, now was a good time to do it. What made the incident strange was that the journalist didn't think it was anything to do with saying his farewells to Diamond but to write it up, so he politely declined.'

It was Dominic who, after his death, edited his columns into a book that would accompany his 'uncomplimentary view of complementary medicine' called *Snake Oil and Other Preoccupations*. In the introduction Dominic describes why he felt he had to finish what John had been unable to. 'John's study on the day after his death presented an almost unbearably poignant sight; his computer screen still switched on, and there, flickering, as if with an extinguished intelligence, the last completed words of his book before he was rushed to hospital: "Let me explain." For once he never did.'

We all know that in reality the screensaver would have clicked in by that time, but it's an interesting story and perhaps tells more about the complicit packaging of a life for public consumption than it does about the relationships between the players. Nigella has said that she learned early on to distinguish between her private and public self. Perhaps the men around her at this time weren't quite so able to make that distinction.

Nigella limited the information made available to the outside world, while keeping it real. 'He's not feeling great at the moment,' she told the press six months before he died. 'He has more mood swings and other people's embarrassment is difficult. I can understand what John said, but other people can't. They don't want to admit it, so they nod or pretend, and that he finds hard.' Women, she said, gave him more time, listened harder and were more likely to get there in the end. 'I think men are much more squeamish and frightened of the disease and don't know how to deal with it.' The children were his greatest leveller, 'Though very cleverly when he's telling them off they can pretend not to understand, which is wonderful and normal,' Nigella said. Bruno had never heard his father speak any differently, and Cosima, unaware of the etiquette of terminal illness, would shout 'What?' with nothing more than sheer irritation if she didn't understand him at first.

John was in the car one day listening to Radio 4 when he

recognized a voice he knew from somewhere. Then he realized that it was himself, a pre-cancerous version of who he was now. He told his readers about how ungrateful that man had been: 'He was the one who didn't realize what a boon an unimpaired voice was, who ate his food without stopping to think about its remarkable flavor, who was criminally profligate with words, who took his wife and children and friends for granted – in short who didn't know he was living.'

Losing his voice drove John ever harder to express himself in his written words, and by the time he died he was writing five different columns a week, he had published a bestselling book on cancer and had made the documentary. A play written by his friend, Victoria Coren, *A Lump in My Throat*, based on his column, was next, creating a veritable industry. As John himself said, 'What next – souvenir coffee mugs?'

His column in *The Times* charted his illness, engaging the reader in his thought processes from the *carpe diem* attitude he adopted which spurred him into buying yet another Harley ('What's Nigella going to say?' he wrote. 'Tell me it's dangerous, that I'll kill myself on it?'), to his diatribe against holistic medicine. He must have loved the fact that his namesake, a Dr John Diamond, is a pioneering figure in alternative and holistic medicine, even if time didn't allow him to invite him to the launch of *Snake Oil and Other Preoccupations*.

His friend, the *Observer*'s Jay Rayner, noticed that in a cruel irony 'the illness that eventually ended John Diamond's life was also, professionally, the very making of him. He was successful before, of course. He was well known around media London as the master of the quickly delivered newspaper opinion piece, first person or otherwise, to a tight deadline. As he continued to chart the course of his illness, through treatment to terminal diagnosis and beyond, there was a growing realization among both readers and editors alike that his immense facility for language, previously expended for the most part on the smallest of domestic issues, had disguised a writer of immense talent and skill.'

Nigella, however, was sceptical about the authenticity of his column. 'I think in a terrible way writing the column stopped him really accepting the situation. It seemed like a way of facing the truth, but it wasn't at all. On the other hand, it's what kept him going for so long. It gave him a voice when he didn't have speech.' He would listen to her advice, and if she felt he was giving too much away, or that the children might be affected in some way, he would edit his copy.

He was writing prolifically and often jauntily in his columns about the illness, and it wasn't just out of the frustration at being silenced. This was his livelihood. His broadcasting career was over, he was still a father of two and husband of a potential goldmine. With an uncertain future of his own, he hatched a plot. Nigella had received praise for her food columns in *Vogue* and had had twelve years of experience eating out for the *Spectator*. She was mad about food, spending more time in Italian delis than most people spend in their own kitchens. She should write a book about food, he suggested. But Nigella wasn't convinced. She had come from a publishing background, and while columns were one thing writing a book which might be judged by her contemporaries was one of her biggest fears.

It was the combined might of literary agent Ed Victor and

John Diamond that tied Nigella to her computer to write *How to Eat*. Victor had already signed authors such as Erica Jong, Jack Higgins, Frederick Forsyth, Douglas Adams, Marie Helvin, Larry King, Sir Ranulph Fiennes and even Nigella's ex's wife, Kathy Lette (which possibly accounts for Kathy's appearances at Nigella's book launches). He was recently reported as being number two on the list of 'the most invited people in London', second only to Sir Elton John. Even his weight loss book *The Obvious Diet* details tips from his celebrity pals such as Mel Brooks and Anne Bancroft ('We keep our upper bodies in good shape by having a terrible fist fight every day'); Tina Brown ('The meat or fish on my plate should be no bigger than a deck of cards') and Ken Follett ('Never eat when you're not hungry, no matter how impolite you feel'). Nigella said in the foreword to *The Obvious Diet* that the book shares 'the giddy virtues of its author: it's lively, insistently pleasure-seeking and absurdly encouraging'. Who else could have become her literary agent?

Astonishingly, by November 1999 Ed Victor had also been diagnosed with cancer, this time chronic lymphocytic leukaemia. After being rushed into intensive care in New York in 2002, where he nearly died, he is now back at work. Nigella – or Typhoid Mary, as she increasingly saw herself and who had by this time formed a close friendship with Victor – must have felt that there were few hiding places.

To imagine that just anyone could pick up an agent like Victor is to misunderstand who Nigella already was in 1998. She may have thought of herself as simply a jobbing journalist, but her husband was out fishing in very big pools, and was bringing home a serious catch from his Scrabble games and evenings at the Groucho Club. 'People tend to come to me by recommendation, by friends, by other clients, or by me going to a party and running into someone,' Victor told the *Guardian*'s Tim Dowling. 'The reason I took on Josephine Hart is I was having dinner with her husband Maurice Saatchi, now Lord Saatchi, and her, and Maurice said, very famously, "Josephine's writing a novel." '

'If you don't find that a particularly helpful example, you're not alone,' wrote Dowling. 'When he was giving a talk at the Hay literary festival alongside Hart, somebody raised his hand and asked, "If I'm not at a party or a dinner with you, how do I get my manuscript to you?" Victor's answer was, "You don't." ' Nigella didn't either. Victor came to her. After a particularly long lunch one day with Nigella and John, Victor called her. 'He said to me: "Do me a favor, just write a book based on everything we've just talked about," ' Nigella told Tamasin Day-Lewis. ' "Don't think about it. If you're too frightened or too self-conscious, it won't work." ' She realized that with John ill and the children still in need of a full-time mother (and nanny) at home, it wasn't a bad option. 'I can be here for their tea and work on a book,' she said.

She was pregnant when she signed the contract for *How to Eat*, and had only written three chapters by the time she had Bruno. 'Then I stopped writing. I was inside that lovely newborn baby bubble. Then suddenly there was a deadline, so on December 28th I sat down and just wrote for six weeks. A chapter a week.'

It took her into a work frenzy that offered a completely new distraction for both her and John. 'I can't plan ahead,' she said at the time. 'I sometimes find it hard to sleep so I am often in the kitchen at two in the morning, doing something like sieving pumpkins or lying in bed wondering if mushrooms would make a dish more delicious. I need to be busy; if I have learned anything from experience, it's the need to distance myself.'

The title *How to Eat* was John's attempt at irony. 'He's got to learn how to eat again,' Nigella told Day-Lewis. 'His taste buds have mostly gone. I made him some custard the other day, but he doesn't appear at meals at the moment. But it's important that I cook for the children, and it suits me to eat at five o'clock with them. Otherwise there wouldn't be a family meal.'

It wasn't just John's cancer that was driving her. 'I wouldn't have written *How to Eat* if my mother and Thomasina hadn't died,' she told Olivia Lichtenstein in *Eve* magazine. 'It was a kind of memorial to them, a way of continuing my conversation with them.' 'Cooking is not simply a process of arcane rituals passed from mother to daughter,' she wrote in her *Vogue* column. 'After all, much better cooks than I have had mothers who can't cook. But it's hard for me not to idealize that particular relationship, one that for me is defined by loss. But writing the book helped; it answered that urgent need to remember, to name, to celebrate.'

How to Eat explained the pleasures and principles of good food to a world of food lovers, with 350 simple recipes designed to give us the skills of our grandmothers. Tips on how to make home-made mayonnaise, stock and pastry dough, ideas about what to do with leftovers, what to freeze and even low-fat menus made us believe that we could knock up a Sunday lunch or a kids' supper without resorting to a single packet. And best of all, Nigella was there with us, a mentor guiding and advising and daring us to free our inner chefs.

'There's a reason why this book is called *How to Eat* rather than *How to Cook*,' wrote Nigella. 'It's a simple one: although it's possible to love eating without being able to cook, I don't believe you can ever really cook unless you love eating. Such love, of course, is not something which can be taught, but it can be conveyed – and maybe that's the point.'

Nigella was probably never intending to broaden her appeal beyond the middle-class, double-income, urban types who shared her lifestyle of the time, and it must have taken a leap of faith for her publishers, Chatto & Windus, to give her free rein. The compromise came in her introduction. 'I have a job – another job, that is, as an ordinary working journalist – and two children, one of whom was born during the writing of this book,' she wrote in an attempt to explain her position and evoke an empathy that she might not have won as a restaurant critic for *Vogue* or daughter of an heiress and a former Chancellor. 'And during the book's gestation,' she went on, 'I would sometimes plan to cook some wonderful something or other, then work out a recipe, apply myself in anticipatory fantasy to it, write out the shopping list, plan the dinner – and then find that when it came down to it I just didn't have the energy. Anything that was too hard, too fiddly, filled me with dread and panic or, even if attempted, didn't work or was unreasonably demanding, has not found its way in here. The people who read me have got jobs and families and my book is about how to cook in real life. I don't set myself up as an expert.

When friends ring and ask me how to cook something, I haven't necessarily got the answer, but I probably know where to find it quicker than them.'

Cooking for her had become a homage to her mother and the childhood she missed out on. She could reinvent the kitchen of her youth, without the 'atmosphering' and with an idealized version of her mother this time, and allow herself to relive her childhood in the way she knew best – in books. 'Although it's possibly not the same as hers,' she wrote in *Vogue* about her style of cooking, 'it is from her that I learned to trust it. And that's what cooking is or should be.'

How to Eat was launched in autumn 1998, along with more chefs' cookbooks than the shelves could hold. Alistair Little, Simon Hopkinson, Gary Rhodes, Raymond Blanc, Jean-Christophe Novelli, Madhur Jaffrey, Sue Lawrence, Loyd Grossman, Jennifer Patterson and Clarissa Dickson Wright, Sybil Kapoor, Antonio Carluccio, Antony Worrall-Thompson, Nigel Slater and Delia Smith were among those ready-wrapped for the Christmas tree that year.

In spite of the competition, *How to Eat* was an enormous success and was voted Illustrated Book of the Year at the British Book Awards in 1998. Her current editor at Chatto, Alison Samuel, said that she 'persuaded a new generation how to cook and changed the way we eat'. The food press (many of whom were Nigella's friends) salivated at the intelligent prose and choice of recipes. 'Nigella Lawson is, whisks down, Britain's funniest and sexiest food writer,' wrote Richard Story in *Vogue*, 'a raconteur who is delicious whether detailing every step on the way towards a heavenly roast chicken and root vegetable couscous or explaining why "cooking is not just about joining the dots".' 'Nigella Lawson is one of the best and most influential of British food writers,' pronounced Ruth Rogers (whose own book, *The River Café Cook Book*, carries a strikingly similar endorsement from her pal Nigella; 'It's a seminal book from a seminal restaurant. I could cook my way through this book forever.').

'Nigella Lawson has long been among the most realistic as well as the most readable of writers on food,' wrote Nick Wroe. 'Her description of a three-star dinner really is a good second best to actually eating it yourself. But equally she knows the inestimable value of a bacon sandwich on sliced white. But most of all Lawson is a greedy eater who knows about food and can write like an angel. "I hate the new-age voodoo about eating," she declares. "The notion that foods are either harmful or healing, that a good diet makes you a good person." Hurrah! *How to Eat* is the perfect book for anyone who knows that food is more than fuel.'

'It is a measure of the change in status of the cookbook, and the breed of writer often to be found writing it, that at the recent launch of Nigella Lawson's book *How to Eat*, novelists outweighed food writers by a considerable margin,' wrote Tamasin Day-Lewis. 'The glamorousness of the occasion was offset by an unexpectedly familial cosiness, which the author was clearly enjoying.'

She fell into a safety net of TV cookery programs with accompanying books, rising supermarket sales in gourmet goods and fine wines, and a growing confidence in the kitchens of Britain. The world had been getting smaller over the past ten years, and the yuppy culture encouraged by

Thatcher and Lawson encouraged people to travel the world on expense accounts and cheaper air fares. Travel had introduced us to cities such as New York, San Francisco, Melbourne and Sydney where immigrants had brought their comfort food from the old countries. From Asia came smells and flavours like lemongrass and galangal, and we were flying into Heathrow from LA with the memory of last night's business dinner confusing our brains. Was that really raspberries stuffed in that chicken? People travelled, and so did food. More interestingly, so did ideas.

Our interest in food may have been growing, but Nigella told us in *How to Eat* that it was all the wrong way around. 'Cooking is best learned at your own stove; you learn by watching and by doing ... The great chefs of France and Italy learn about food at home; what they do later in the restaurants that make them famous is use what they have learned. They build on it, start elaborating.' She warned us that if we weren't careful, we'd become a culture of 'culinary mimics', with no 'authentic language' of our own. Learn your grammar first, she scolded, the basics, and then break the rules.

The supermarket wine racks were the center of the British revolution. While Marco Pierre White was wielding his meat cleaver for the tabloids in the UK, Australia was reinventing itself as the center of fusion and New York's bagel bars were becoming even hipper than LA's noodle bars, Sainsbury's in particular was quietly dispatching its wine buyers to bring in a new range of wines to lure this new generation of yuppies back home.

With affordable fine wines to drink at home, newspapers began to trumpet the rise of the dinner party as a new social phenomenon, and a new generation of young men – also inspired by Jamie Oliver – and women realized that cooking was sexy.

CHAPTER EIGHT

Nigella Bites

The table was laid for a new TV cook. TV is a barometer of British culinary trends, and TV producers, fed on a diet of *nouvelle cuisine* in the 1980s, were coming up with a recipe for change: take an interest in food and a hole in a national soul, they prescribed. Add some exotic spices, a dash of aspiration and a few sexy chefs with increasingly large bank accounts. Add some nice middle-class cooks, tear off a handful of Cockney rhyming slang and stir in a few of those celebrity chefs with the bulging wallets, and bring to the boil on a prime-time television show. Sprinkle in a little aspiration (a nice kitchen, a surfing holiday or a stunning Cornwall landscape – according to taste) and simmer while they write the books to go with the TV series. Spoon a generous helping of opportunity on a bed of talent, making sure it doesn't wilt before serving.

Producers had been trying to lure the 'raven-haired beauty', the 'handsome' daughter of the Chancellor who had been reluctantly paraded by the press into the limelight since her mid-twenties. TV producer, Janice Gabriel was working on an LWT chat show with Melvyn Bragg in the mid-1980s, and approached her to appear as a pundit. 'She was writing for the *Evening Standard* at the time,' Gabriel said. 'Everyone wanted her because she was glamorous, bright and famous as the daughter of the Chancellor. Melvyn thought she was fantastic and really wanted her on the show. When I phoned her, she flatly turned it down. She said, "Oh my God, me? On television? Oh no. I couldn't possibly." She didn't think of herself in that way at all. Melvyn was really disappointed.'

By the time she had made a guest appearance on her friend Nigel Slater's show ten years later, the light bulbs popping in the production offices of Channel Four were enough to light up the whole of London. From here, the idea of Nigella's TV career wasn't a question of 'if', but 'when'. The 'when' was when John and Nigella made their way to the offices of Kudos, producers of the Channel's *TV Dinners* with Hugh Fearnley-Whittingstall (infamous for the dubious TV first of using a placenta in a recipe). They went there with an idea for a TV show and a pretty clear understanding of Nigella's potential.

While *How to Eat* could never be as seminal a work as *Mrs Beeton's Book of Household Management* had been for our mothers' and grandmothers' generations, it told stories to a new wave of home cooks and promised a certain kind of lifestyle. The time was right for a new TV chef, but this time we needed something far more sophisticated than before. 'We'd had Delia,' said Janice, now a senior producer at Kudos. 'We'd had Ainslie and Gary Rhodes, Keith Floyd and Rick Stein. It was the time when Jamie had been on with *Naked*

Chef and food had gone through the roof. Everyone wanted to know who was going to be the next Jamie. He'd done the lifestyle show, and Nigella offered something for the slightly older, aspirational, family-oriented viewer. Everyone thought she would be a success. There was no doubt. It was partly her pedigree, partly the *Vogue* column, partly because the book had been very successful and was very easy to turn into TV; it was a beautifully written book and evoked a lifestyle. She seemed to be so full of stories.'

Janice and her team went to see Nigella and John at home with Ben Frow, then Commissioning Editor at Channel Four. 'He'd seen her on the Nigel Slater program and decided that she had something. He was very clever from the outset and decided that he wanted her to be a Channel Four person. Everyone thought that there hadn't been a successful, *sexy* woman in food, and there was absolutely a place for someone like Nigella to succeed, for moms to want to be like her. I think women wanted the package that was Nigella. When you meet someone like Nigella, she's incredibly naturally beautiful. She has a beautiful face, gorgeous eyes and hair, and you look at her and think, Yes, she's gorgeous, but she's not necessarily threatening. When we first met her to discuss *Nigella Bites* she dealt with make-up like everyone else does, and she talked a bit about electrolysis on her legs like we all do, but she wasn't over-obsessed with make-up, and her nails were really ordinary – she didn't do anything special with them. She was a bit like a rushed mom. She had so many things to do that she didn't necessarily focus on her appearance. We felt that people would identify with her on lots of different levels. In spite of everything that was happening in her life, she could sit down and still turn out all these amazing dishes in her book. On that level you thought, "Yes she'd be a success." '

It takes a certain kind of ego to want to be a TV presenter. Nigella has talked about being addicted to fear. 'I am fearful,' she said, 'so I do something. It's not that I'm a workaholic, it's rather that I like to tread the precarious line between boredom and fear. I need to be frightened of things. I hate it, but I must need it, because it's what I do.' Her fear of cameras, she told Sally Vincent in the *Guardian*, was about her 'fear of disappointment that the image will not correspond with your idea of yourself'. This, she said, was why she began 'vamping in front of cameras, dressing up in kitsch costumes, thinking to herself, "Hey, it's not my fault my cleavage starts under my nose. Twenty years ago I would have disapproved of myself, but now I think, 'Well, make the most of it, it won't last much longer.' " Yet behind the bravado, the secret self remains unseen. "That's the joke." '

In 1999 Nigella wasn't as convinced as her husband was that what he saw as a gay man trapped in Nigella's body who vamped around at home would translate to the TV screens, or that her act would make her a star. Janice said that she was 'quite humble about the whole thing. When we had our first meetings, she wasn't very interested in how she would look on screen. She was interested in being girly with the girls and looking after the men.'

There was another driving force. Her mother may have been an heiress, but she also lost a lot and left only £100,000 between the four children. 'Money is so not my sphere,' Nigella said, 'but I've been self-supporting for a long time.' Money might not have been her sphere, but it was John's. With a successful book under Nigella's belt, John was on a mission to turn her into the kind of star who would earn £4 million from her cooking empire within the next three years. He'd always been more focused than she was on working his way towards the kind of life that would give him money, power and glamour, writing and broadcasting about just about anything for just about anyone who would pay him. Driven he certainly was, but when he became a father he shifted into top gear. When cancer struck he became turbo-charged.

Was John another Svengali figure, a powerful and imaginative mentor like Ed Victor, or simply a husband urging her to make the most of herself? 'I'm sure that it wasn't as conscious as that,' Christopher Silvester said. 'I really think that it was a natural process. John had tremendous *chutzpah* and Nigella was lacking in that kind of confidence. I'm sure that John would have actively encouraged her to do TV, and if she had any doubts he would have dispelled them.'

Janice disagreed. 'When we started to do the pilot for *Nigella Bites*, it was driven by John. He couldn't talk – but he would come in and out to check on things. He seemed very separate at that time. I think she was his brand. Maybe he saw her in a way she didn't see herself. That was probably quite key. He was a smart man, he saw the potential, and he'd seen how his friends had responded to her. She was probably quite a rare bird in the world that she existed in.'

Director Bruce Goodison said that John simply wanted her to make the most of herself and was very encouraging. 'You didn't get the sense of any cynicism about making her into a star, but there was a lot of preparation for what would happen after he died. She would always defer to him. She asked his opinion about everything, but she asked a lot of people too. It's a complex psychological area for her. She is a reluctant public face, but ambitious at the same time – although I'm not sure that she is any more. She really believed in her book and she wanted to make the most of it, and John really supported her in that.'

Janice said there was a lot of talk about money. 'They even used their own kitchen so they could get a location fee,' she said. 'She described it as a mess, but it was very ordinary. It was a typical middle-class kitchen, with fifties cupboards which I think she'd had put in herself. It was quite stylish. She had a huge American fridge and it was exactly like she has in the series, with all these little bags of things slotted away. But she'd already had the kitchen set up professionally in some ways because she'd already done the book. All the recipes for *How to Eat* had been done in that kitchen.'

As an outsider, Janice said that it felt a bit odd that they were so money-oriented. 'You thought they must have a lot of money. I think it must have been to prepare Nigella for what was about to come. I didn't ever hear her talk about money for herself. I wonder if that transfer to Saatchi so quickly was about that need for her to have a man to look after her. I think she needs that. She didn't seem to have that confidence without it.'

Even the choice of production companies was theirs, something that usually the broadcaster would select. 'Kudos established her, but for some reason Channel Four put it out to tender and we all had to provide program ideas,' said Janice. 'But Nigella met with Fi Cotter Craig and Rachel

Purnell (executive producers at Pacific Televison) herself and liked the fact that they were women and quite strong, so the first series was made with them.' They brought in director Bruce Goodison to assemble the team for their pilot. 'I didn't want to do food,' he said. 'I'd been offered the Jamie Oliver series but turned it down, but I was persuaded to go and see Nigella by Fi and Rachel and of course I fell in love with her. She's unbelievably charming and persuasive. I was very drawn into Nigella's world and got very attached to everybody. I spent a lot of time hanging out at the house with her and John, stayed over for dinner a lot, and we came up with some great ideas for the show.'

Most of those ideas didn't make it on to the screen, although Bruce said he noticed that a lot of what they shot for the pilot appeared in the first series. 'My idea was to ignore the recipes and do a lifestyle show – a window into the world of Nigella,' he said. 'She was really worried that people would think she was too posh. I said, "Well, you *are* posh, but that doesn't mean that you're not terribly charming." She'd had a lot of tragedy in her life, and that gave her something that people could relate to. I wanted it to be about eating rather than cooking, with people dropping in for anything from leftovers to a fancy dinner. I wanted to open it up and make it about sociability, about life around the kitchen as the nucleus of the family. Everything moves around that. It's a lovely way of bringing the whole family in. It was about a woman who cooks while a bloke is dying of cancer, where everyone who came into the house is a character. It was more like an Almodóvar film than a cookery program.'

Nigella, John and Bruce had a great time playing with

ideas for the show. With John as Associate Producer and their own company MYC co-producing, this was work they could do down the pub. 'I remember asking John what he wanted to drink,' Bruce said, 'and he asked for a pint of Guinness. I thought, "Oh my Lord, how's he going to do this?" and he got this syringe out and filled it up.'

They played with the idea of giving the camera to John and Nigella. 'They'd already made a film in their house,' said Bruce, referring to Olivia Lichtenstein's *Tongue Tied* for the BBC, 'and so they were very camera aware. The idea was to have the camera filming their life twenty-four hours a day, catching Nigella in bed reading about baking tins which would be flown in from America, John grumbling around the house writing notes. You can't help being sucked into her world. They're all so charming.'

'Nigella and John loved the ideas,' Bruce said, 'but I think that Channel Four wanted more of the food porn show; they wanted a fancy footwear goddess doing food porn.' Eventually they decided that Neville Kidd would hold the camera and that Nigella would get on with her cooking as naturally as is possible with a crew watching your every move. 'I told her to get on with what she was doing with the food and occasionally look to camera,' Bruce said. 'A bit like the Jamie Oliver series, I wanted her to talk to her assistant, to me behind the camera so that you had a feeling that there was another presence there.'

Her assistant was a home economist, Hettie Potter, the silent partner who worked on the science of the food for all the TV shows and the books. 'I don't think she could have done it without her,' an observer said. 'I think if you're a woman, it's quite important to be part of the court of Nigella, to respond in the right way.' Nigella said that it was a meeting of soulmates. 'I met her on a set and I could sense her sadness – her mother had just died – so I asked her to come and work with me. She's become like a sister. We cook together, just as I used to with Thomasina, and she tells me when to stop. "You get some rest now and we'll carry on with that tomorrow," she says to me. And I do.' She thanked her in her book *Feast* for her 'bolstering and affectionate efficiency' and as someone who 'has cooked with me, cared for me, driven me mad and kept me sane'.

Hettie's job on the pilot was to prepare the food for the filming, to source the ingredients and to keep the atmosphere light. 'She was very funny, a regular kind of person,' said Bruce. 'She was the real powerhouse of the series. The journey of making anything was the fun bit. I remember her making a cake which didn't turn out properly. It sagged in the middle, but it was fun to make. That's what it was like a lot of the time.' David Edgar, who took over as producer, explained how they worked together for the show: 'We would work with Nigella and Hettie to choose the recipes which would provide the balance of the episode, and then they would work them out before Nigella cooked them for the camera.'

Hettie became more than her TV partner. When the *Guardian* journalist Simon Hattenstone went to interview Nigella, he reported that he was humbled to be eating chicken cooked by such a fair hand. 'Nothing to do with me,' Nigella told him, attributing it to Hettie, who was working downstairs in the Shepherd's Bush home she used for the TV series, and which, since she and the children had moved out, had become her younger sister Horatia's new home. Simon felt that he should pass on the compliment, to tell Hettie what a good cook she is, but was told not to worry. 'She's confident. She knows she is.' 'But it's nice to be told you're good, isn't it?' insisted Simon. 'I've already thanked her profusely,' Nigella told him firmly.

Hettie and the female team of executive producers fussed over Nigella's outfits while the men built a TV set out of an urban basement kitchen. TV is a medium that presents what it wants you to see, yet it can't help adding a good few pounds to any presenter. It's quite a feat to cover your really curvy bits. I sneakily asked Janice just how big her bottom really is. 'I never saw her bottom half,' she said. 'She always wore trousers or long skirts. I never saw her ankles. We dressed her for the pilot, and I think we got a couple of outfits from Whistles, but she asked us only to get tops and she kept her black bottoms on. She would say that she had tree trunk legs and that she had really big thighs but she disguised it really well because she's really slender on top. Her hands, her shoulders, her neck are really quite delicate. She's the classic hourglass shape with a tiny top.'

'People think that I'm a big girl, but I'm a person with a very small build and a lot of flesh' she told Nina Myskow in the *Mirror*. 'I've varied between 7 stone 10 lbs and 13 1/2 stone when Cosima was born. I was unhappy then. I'm now a shadow under 10 stone and perfectly happy. It's a good stone heavier than a lot of women want to be at my height – I'm 5'7".' In the past, she said that she's leaned towards anorexia and bulimia, but like most foodies she couldn't quite be bothered in the end. She even tried diet pills but found that they made her more depressed, and the only thing that would cheer her up was a good meal. 'I don't mind the fact that I'm not lean and firm,' Nigella said, 'and I'm probably meant to. I think that you take it for granted if you're female that if you've got wide hips or something like that it's not only the most terrible aesthetic disaster, but also some kind of moral failing.' 'I do give up carbohydrates,' she told Brian Vine, 'but I've sometimes lost weight by eating everything – just not in such huge amounts. I have to remind myself that I'm not going to be sent away with no food ever again if I don't finish everything on my plate. On the other hand, I don't have a fantasy to wear a very tight pair of jeans with my belly showing. I'm bosomy and bottomy with quite a small waist – that's what I am.'

She asked Bruce Goodison to tell her if she looked fat. 'Nobody else cared, but she didn't want to look fat or frumpy,' he said. 'She's a big girl, Rubensesque.' She was asking the wrong sex. 'Skinny doesn't work for me in the kitchen anyway,' said Bruce. 'And there were plenty of executive producers around who made her look positively lithe.' It didn't stop her getting a personal trainer to take her for runs on a regular basis. 'He came over most days,' said Bruce.

It was Bruce and John who spotted the vamp in her, and encouraged it to come on out and take a bow. 'I was absolutely upfront with her about the fact that we were making gastro-porn,' said Bruce. 'I'd stop the tape and ask her to take more time licking the cream off the strawberry, or to whip eggs more sensually. I made no bones about it.' She was a natural. 'She's a very sexy woman,' Bruce smiled. 'She's creamy. With warm chocolate all over.' But it wasn't just about flirting with a sexy director who you know is mad about you. 'It's a matter of trust when you ask someone to do something like that,' he explained, 'and she trusted me not to take it into the realm of parody. I think that did happen by the third series [*Forever Summer*] and you could see that she just wasn't comfortable with it.'

Some say that it was the desire to gain more control that led to a new production company being called in during the first series, while others report a spat between the powerful trio of women currently running the show. 'John was driving things at this time,' David Edgar, producer at Flashback Productions, said. 'We were called in to meet with her people during the first series – her TV agent Jaquie Drewe and I think Ed Victor was there. And we were asked to make the new series. In terms of control, there was no difference in our relationship with MYC TV [Nigella and John's company] and Pacific's. I think it had more to do with the relationships involved. I knew Ben Warwick [the director on the first and second series, and the man, incidentally, who directed the River Café series in which a chirpy young Cockney sous-chef shot to fame] and it was expected that he would continue to direct. As a producer, my job is to support her, to offer empathy. We really got on.'

Nigella had been trained to flirt from the cradle, and by the age of fourteen she would have learned the art of small talk and turning her parents' cocktail parties from achingly dull endurance tests into a training ground for her own skills, using wit and wiles to make middle-aged men weak at the knees before flitting off to chat up the next diplomat or major-general. She would have learned her social graces by osmosis and peer group pressure, taking on her mother's title as queen of the flirt and terrifying most men with her show-stopping combination of sharp intellect and Nefertiti looks. Her crew on *Nigella Bites* was almost all men.

David Edgar admits he was intimidated when he went to talk to her about the new series he was to take on. 'I went down to her kitchen and I was very nervous with her,' he said. 'I felt I was in the presence of someone who's very bright and will pick you up on anything you say. But after we'd been talking for some time, she turned round and said, '"How do *you* see me?" I told her, "Well, you're a posh girl who can cook, and who, frankly is a bit of a babe. At the moment, that's all I know." I realized that this was rather a two-dimensional view. There's an awful lot more to her. She's had the most remarkably privileged background, yet she has this extraordinary line in common sense. She wouldn't be out of place having a cup of tea with a bunch of blokes digging up the roads.'

Bruce Goodison agrees. 'I remember going to Sainsbury's with Nigella. We were filming her there and she seemed so natural. She knew everyone and everyone knew her. It was the same at the butchers (Lidgate's, her family butcher in Notting Hill). And there was absolutely no division between her and the crew at all.' Those who spend any amount of time with her also comment on her fragility, something that can melt the hardest heart. 'She was self-deprecating and humble, slightly closed and sweet,' said Janice. 'Fawn-like is a good description. She had a fragility which protected her from women as well. You kind of allowed her to be like that.'

The Flashback crew loved her. And she loved them, flirting outrageously with them, watching them play with her kids and with her, and relaxing enough with them to let the Queen of Gastro-porn strut her stuff. Cracking eggs and allowing the whites to dribble slowly through her fingers, throwing her head back and dangling pasta over her outstretched tongue, and coming up with lines like 'You've got to feel more relaxed at the end of the day after a bit of squelching and squeezing like this,' before tipping a squid into her open mouth. This was *fun*. The effect on the camera was electric: slapping on a pair of gynaecologist's gloves to massage a beetroot, she gave her best head-down, eyes-up Diana look to camera and said naughtily, 'Don't worry, Matron will be *very* gentle with you.'

Watch anyone mixing together the ingredients to make a sweet, and they will lick the bowl. And very possibly close their eyes and sigh. And yes, very possibly they are having just as much fun with a mixing bowl as they do in the bedroom. But to do it on TV, to take a moment to savour the pure bliss of creamed chocolate, butter and sugar was perceived as an outrageous act of self-satisfaction and left grown men dribbling into their TV dinners. Gastro-porn, a term invented by Nigella ('as a pre-emptive strike'), it was decided by the press, was Nigella's unique selling point, her USP. 'I can only be a version of me,' Nigella said as she leafed through the press cuttings. 'I'm probably thought of as more knowing and coquettish than I mean to be. I have a sense of camp, although it never comes over as that, and I'm hamstrung by my irony.'

Most of her male viewers were far too distracted to bother with the irony, and Nigella's entrance on to the world stage encouraged more adjectives to fly off keyboards than newspapers and magazines had seen in decades. Apparently bets were laid among men's magazines as to the most pornographic copy that any of them could get away with.

Hers was a culinary come-on that had critics salivating over their copy. 'She looks like the voluptuous star of a Fellini film who has come unstuck in time and found herself transplanted from Rome circa 1960 to present-day Shepherd's Bush,' sighed *GQ*'s Alex Bilmes in January 2001. 'A statuesque, olive-skinned, doe-eyed, pouty-mouthed bella signora with long, dark, straggly hair and English teeth, beamed across time and space to entrance us with her upper-crust stove-side manner and alluring looks. When I tell her how sexy the *GQ* staff find her, and how jealous they are that she's cooking me lunch on this otherwise unremarkable Friday, with the rain pitter-pattering politely on her conservatory roof and the sweet smell of baking muffins wafting gently through the room, she offers only an embarrassed giggle and asks simply that I don't "disabuse them" of their opinion. "I think it's that men don't just want to look at thin girls," she said of the sex-symbol status at which she has arrived comparatively late in life. "The only man who's ever told me to lose weight was a boyfriend I had who turned out to be gay." '

'According to the *Malleus Malificarum*, a 15th-century tract on diabolism, the devil may one day come among us in female form,' wrote Nigel Farndale in the *Telegraph*. 'A raven-haired succubus, that sort of thing. Watching the dark-eyed, pouty, bosomy Nigella ... is to be reminded of this she-devil theory ... Instead of horns, this she-devil has curlers jutting from her hair. Where a devilish tail might be, there's a microphone wire. It runs up her back and emerges from the collar of her pale green silk pyjamas. She is wearing these because she's filming a scene in which she raids her fridge for a midnight snack. Are silk pyjamas what she really sleeps in? "No," she said crisply, raising one eyebrow. "I don't wear anything in bed. But I'm not ready for a nude scene quite yet." '

'I do feel that food is quite sexy, and when I'm talking to a camera it is quite intimate,' Nigella told Sue Lawley on *Desert Island Discs* before deflating any surging male emotions with, 'I feel like I'm talking to a sister or a friend.' Sally Vincent was one journalist who recognized the irony, and welcomed her all-woman approach to cooking. 'In these days of television foodery, it is interesting to observe that we are instructed in our food preparation by bad-tempered men or well-scrubbed women who have in common a tendency to be didactic and exacting, as though they're going to set a test at the end to see if you were listening. Then along comes Lawson, who gets it all down herself and lets her hair trail in the soup. More singularly, she seems to be enjoying herself.'

She took a copy of Jonathan Coe's novel, *The Closed Circle*, to show Nigella. In it the would-be adulterous husband is ironing his shirt in front of a cookery show on television. Vincent described the scene. 'He sees an implausibly glamorous young woman, living in an implausibly elegant house, preparing delicious morsels of food while tossing her hair, pouting seductively at the camera and licking traces of butter and sauce off her fingers in a manner so explicitly suggestive of oral sex that he found himself getting an erection while ironing his cuffs for the fifth time. Coe does not sully his prose with unnecessary information, and his purveyor of gastro-eroticism is not named. We know who it is, though. More to the point, she knows.'

Vincent asked her if she'd seen this book. 'She said she hadn't. She took my copy ... and read it through with the concentrated gravity of one who began her working life as a serious literary critic. She closed the book and set it down with a barely audible sigh. No comment. Later, by way of an acknowledgement, she said, "I am not young." So far as she is concerned that is a matter of fact; 44 is not young. As for the rest of it, she cannot possibly be responsible for what goes on in the eyes, hearts, minds and groins of her beholders. There is nothing she can do about it but softly sigh and smile a brave and odontologically perfect smile. She is denying her collusion in this coquettish game. "I suppose I am naïve," she said. "I play into the hands of my detractors." '

Inevitably, the press pitched her against the British kitchen queen Delia Smith, and Nigella relished the opportunity to invite her alter ego to deal with it. Christopher Silvester remembers watching her on *Have I Got News for You*. 'She wore a T-shirt with the word "Delia" inscribed in glitter. I'm sure it wasn't a real rivalry, but it's a good example of how sharp she is. You know that when the media is playing a game with you, you've got to know how to play the game back. I thought that was a smart move.' The T-shirt was inspired by Madonna, who had recently been in a similar situation, the 'grand dame' pitched against her young pretender, by a British press who were desperate for juicy copy. Madonna, who's always been able to outplay these clumsy press moves, responded by going out in a black T-shirt with the word 'Kylie' written in glamour glitter.

'I have a sense of kitsch and irony, and overcompensate for a sharp side,' Nigella said. 'I've been made to sound much more intimidating than I am, though. I think of myself as a wet walkover.' Nigella was always going to win in the style stakes. But Christopher believes that she had much more to offer than the competition. 'I see that Nigella has more depth than Delia. She's a very good literary and book reviewer – and was very perceptive even at a young age. Some people were very snooty about her food reviews but I thought that they were always well informed and witty and interesting.'

Some critics called her the 'new Diana' – without a hint of irony. She was even voted the third most beautiful woman in the world after Catherine Zeta-Jones and one of the Corrs. 'Did they give them a multiple choice? Did they give them a list that they can choose from?' laughed Nigella when she heard. 'It's so absurdly flattering that it's alarming. I could do without that, without thinking "Oh my God, what about my eye bags?" When we went on vacation, the woman who owned the villa we rented said, "But I was told you were beautiful. It must be the worry." So of course it's flattering but I'm neurotic enough to see the negative in anything positive. It's a great Jewish gift.'

When the TV impersonators added her to their repertoire, Nigella appreciated the joke. 'I think Ronnie Ancona's very good,' she told Andrew Harrison, 'and I do like Jan Ravens in *Dead Ringers* – she's the best, I think. Ronnie always does me very intense and cool, which is funny because I don't think I'm like that at all. I did a shoot yesterday and they had to stop and re-do the make-up because the photographer said I was starting to look like Ronnie Ancona doing Nancy

Dell'Olio.' 'What about Jan Ravens having an orgasm as "Nigella" cleaning the toilet?' he asked her. 'Well, as long as it's funny you can't complain,' she replied. 'I like it. I so didn't realize that I'm like that on TV. I thought I was intimate, but not so ... overtly ... like that. I'm actually the sort of person who doesn't get a *double entendre* and has no idea about that kind of thing.'

Her friends were suitably mocking. 'They come around asking me to lick my fingers or tilt my head back,' she told the *Chicago Times*. 'If they do this too much, they get banned from my kitchen. It's a difficult act to live up to being billed as a sexy chef. I'm fairly relaxed about it because people are always going to try to find something they can use to define you. I view myself as more straightforward than sexy. I'm greedy and I don't hide that. I do what I do because I want to eat.'

Allowing a TV crew into your home is a weird thing to do at the best of times, and for Nigella it was a double-edged sword while John was dying. 'I enjoy making the programs but I'm not keen on those video inserts, wandering around with the children, which are meant to show my life,' she said, and explained why she agreed to let the director have a free rein. 'They needed narrative and a break in the cooking. The children want to be involved rather than not, but they're getting to an age when it wouldn't be right to do it again. It makes me uncomfortable because I don't like being the subject. I'm not a pop star. On the other hand embarrassment is appropriate, especially if you're on TV.' In the real world, juggling the filming, the hospital trips and the everyday family meals was becoming less possible. 'Mimi [Cosima] said to me: "Everyone at school's really jealous because they think you cook us lovely things all the time, but I said, "Oh, she never has time to cook for us," ' Nigella confessed. 'And I heard myself bleating rather weakly, "Oh, but I do sometimes." '

The more mundane aspects of mothering were also proving to be a challenge. As a child, her parents had forced table manners on her, refusing to let her leave the table until she has eaten everything on her plate. 'I'm trying to get stricter, to make them behave better at mealtimes,' she told Brian Vine. 'I'm afraid I got very lax when John was ill. I didn't have the energy for the fight, and I also felt so sorry for them, and John wasn't very connected with their day-to-day care. I found it difficult to get angry with them, and I think they got out of hand. But I am the original voice of no authority.'

The crew became part of her family, with between ten and sixteen weeks of filming at any one time and long hours of filming every day. 'We'd know if any of the family bought a new pair of shoes,' said David Edgar. It was a cosy world of make-believe with a bunch of grown men constantly being slipped a cupcake or two by a Jewish mother in rollers. 'You either eat when you're stressed or you don't eat,' she explained. 'And I eat. When John was first ill, he got much thinner and I put on a lot of weight. Food is a comfort, but the difficulty with comfort food is that it makes you feel awful. You hate yourself the moment you've finished eating. Which is why you carry on, isn't it?' And that's why she started baking. 'You turn yourself into a pusher rather than a user.' Visitors to her house will tell you that even the boiler-man goes home with a package of silver foil containing a little something for the weekend.

Nigel Farndale went to watch Flashback filming *Nigella*

Bites for the *Telegraph*. 'There is a frivolous atmosphere,' he wrote, 'banter among the film crew, mobile phones ringing, the clattering of utensils. Rubber matting has been laid down to protect the floor and, with lights, cameras, cables and monitors cluttering up the place, you can see why Nigella compares the experience to "having the builders in". She removes a tray from her oven, the director says "Cut" and a make-up artist rushes over to even out the skin tones on her manicured hands, in case there are any red marks left by the hot tray. There are a couple of retakes to do before it's a wrap – and the director asks the presenter if she thinks she should be "matronly or camp" for a scene in which she sprinkles pomegranate seeds with her fingers. She opts for sultry: "Mmm. Just look at these beads pouring down like pink rain." Nigella's children – Cosima, seven, and Bruno, four – run in wearing school uniforms, sucking lollies. Their nanny, an Italian, follows. Two Birman cats slink in after her. It's a chaotic scene. Nigella likes it this way. It distracts her.'

The first question most people ask when they meet someone who works with a celebrity is 'What's she really like?', and almost universally those who worked with Nigella will tell you that she is the real deal. 'I don't think she changed very much at all during the process of making her a TV star,' David Edgar said. 'I think she might have grown in confidence, but what you see is what you get with her. Nobody puts words into her mouth. I think I did give her one line once. She'd given me a large piece of chocolate cake to try, and I think I said something like, "That's what I'd call the cake you want to eat when you've just been chucked."' But the process of making a cookery program is slightly more complicated than asking Nigella to cook while the camera watches on. Her famously florid prose was considered over the top and her penchant for 'polysyllabics' ('a Nigella term') was the subject of many a production meeting.

The fascination about the goddess's life, body and background fades into insignificance when she begins to talk about food. No ingredient is added to a dish without a sniff and a sigh and an adjective or two that makes the most humble foods mouth-wateringly desirable; ginger is 'sweet heat', aubergines 'soft and smoky', feta is 'sharp and salty'. The combining of ingredients becomes the 'spicy sweet tangle of flavors' and the smell of a lamb shank welcoming her guests to dinner is an 'aromatic fug'. The colors become vivid: 'The coral of the salmon against the almost psychedelic yellow of the rice'. Even the mundane old button mushroom is given a make-over when mixed with porcini mushrooms. 'Something strange happens to them,' she coos. 'It's as if they respond to the call of the wild and all their mushroomyness returns to them.' 'You should have heard what she said in the first take,' laughed David Edgar when I asked him how she gets away with lines like that. 'I think what she had said at first was something about comparing the mushrooms to Russian Formulism. That's essential Nigella.'

CHAPTER NINE

The picture in the attic

While the magic world of TV was casting its spell over what was once her slovenly Bohemian kitchen, and transforming Nigella into a goddess, a culinary icon for the middle classes, John was upstairs fulfilling his part of their Faustian pact. Turning from the garrulous, funny man he once was into 'a little old man called Albert, Norman or George', as he wrote in his column, losing weight, hair and time, thrashing out his humor – good and bad – on his keyboard into the small hours when sleep would elude him again, John was becoming the picture of Dorian Gray.

'He was incredibly angry a lot of the time,' Nigella told Lynda Lee-Potter. 'But then he had the right to be. I got upset if he did it in front of the children, although they were so understanding. Sometimes now they say, "Do you remember when Daddy broke the door?" ' He had always been someone who could show his anger. 'He's very good at getting cross. He's not a sulker. You don't have to spend all your time thinking, "What's the matter?" '

'John was very angry at the fact that he was dying,' said

Christopher Silvester. 'He was angry about the fact that he had such a perfect life apart from this dreadful illness. He had beautiful children, everything was going well in their careers, and then this cancer came along and ruined everything. The thing that made it appallingly poignant was that he could no longer eat. He could drink, though. He would chuck it straight into his stomach and get drunk. I think he thought, What the hell, I'm going to die anyway.'

Maria McErlane, John's best friend, and his 'blonde wife' as Nigella called her, was also there for him. 'She was much braver than me,' said Nigella. 'She'd say, "John, shut up. You may have terminal cancer but there's no need to be in such a bad mood all the time." I've never been jealous of anyone in my life,' Nigella added in defense of the unique relationship between Maria and John. 'It sounds awful, but I feel when someone gets me, they're not going to *want* anyone else.'

'John did become a bit of a prima donna at the end, but he was the dearest man,' remembers Sarah Johnson. 'He was so warm and so affectionate and so funny. I remember when they lived in North Kensington we went for dinner with my eldest, who was then about two, and John begged me to let him read *The Cat in the Hat*. He said, "I've been waiting for twenty-five years to be able to read this to a little boy." '

John was becoming an observer in his own home, wandering around in an increasingly surreal version of his former life. In June 1999 he wrote: 'I find myself wandering downstairs purposefully when Nigella and her assistant Hettie are in their most vigorous Fanny Cradock modes and pulling hot and reeking pies out of the oven like magicians pulling flags-of-all-nations out of their pockets.' This was the man for whom food had been fuel and who, now that he no longer had taste buds, dreamed of the stuff. Living above a TV studio where he once ate his Cornflakes drove him to distraction. 'I watch things like *Ready Steady Cook* on afternoon TV, and am able momentarily to imagine that I could re-create the dishes for myself. I read cookbooks and the recipe sections of magazines and papers, and the other day I so completely forgot that I am past eating that I chucked a round, hard chocolate into my mouth and then had to do a headstand to stop it choking me.'

When the filming was over for the day and the children were in bed, Nigella would be John's again, understanding the reality of both depression and death. Although she says that she's not sure she ever thought he would actually die, she knew about dying and how to live in each moment, practically, thoughtfully, fully. John's view, as ever, was published in a national newspaper. 'My position is this: I have an apparently terminal disease which doesn't allow me to make any realistic plans for more than a couple of months ahead, a voice which stopped when my cancerous tongue was removed, a diet entirely dependent on the food blender, and a fair to middling amount of pain on most days. To add insult to cancerous injury, I neither feel the need of nor can I discover any comfort in religious faith and I take refuge, legally or otherwise, in no more than the occasional dose of mind-nudging drugs.' Nigella, whom Sarah Johnson describes as 'noble', made no judgements. 'He could be moody and very difficult. You don't have to be a better person because you've got terminal cancer.'

When John was first diagnosed, Nigella refused to let

anyone near her, preferring to take control and to protect the children. 'They take their cue from me. If I'm all right, they're all right,' she said. But when the future was pronounced as inevitably bleak, she called upon her 'wonderful friends'. 'It's been hard, but I have learned to accept it. That people really do want to help.' The world around her also responded with tremendous sympathy; this is a woman well loved by her peers as well as her fans, but for Nigella, the control freak, it was often deeply uncomfortable. 'When things are difficult, it's always people being sympathetic who make it harder. That's when you think, "I'm going to cry," but you don't.' As people she had never met were introduced to her to talk about their respective disasters, and others would ask her with head cocked and already nodding to her unspoken answer, 'How's John?' she began to hole up in Shepherd's Bush. She heeded the words of her dying sister, Thomasina, only a few years earlier, who told her 'I try now to listen only to what people mean, not to what they say.' Everyone meant well, but what was she supposed to say? 'People mean no harm,' she explained. 'If no one can say the right thing, it's because there is no right thing to say.'

She also talked to the press, possibly in a bid to contain the media interest and to control the amount of gossip circulating, but also because the media were the world in which both John and Nigella lived. 'When I found out it wasn't going to be OK,' she said in an interview with Nina Myskow, 'I had this moment of panic. My only experience of cancer was of someone not getting better, and not getting better pretty quickly.' But John was a fighter, and the Royal Marsden's doctors were astonished at how he responded to the many operations. 'I lurch from anxiety to anxiety,' Nigella said in 2000, only a few months before he died. The prognosis at the time was that, although he was fairly well, the cancer would inevitably return. And get worse. 'I don't prepare myself,' she said. 'Having gone through it before I know that there is no way you can ever truly contemplate how awful things are when someone's physical presence is taken away from you.'

When he was told he was to have the rest of his tongue removed, he told Nigella he would kill himself rather than live without speech. 'I said "Please don't. I need you, and the children need you." I just put my arms around him. He was the most gregarious person in the world,' she told the *Mail*. 'It was torture for him to have his voice taken away. Having both his legs amputated would have been better. It's almost impossible to imagine what that pain was like.'

She became his voice. 'It was odd at first having to translate things that I would never say,' she remembers. 'We were very different and I found it hard to repeat crude jokes. It's not that John's a crude person but he might be in a certain situation which would make me blush enormously.'

John had always loved glamour, and as he was dying he threw caution to the wind. This was the man who bought a Rolls Royce days before he died, who had designer suits made as he lost weight. The thinner he got, the more dapper the whistle. Always a champagne socialist, he wasn't going to let the fact that he had to eat and drink through a tube get in the way of his elegant lifestyle, and when an unflinching head waiter responded to his request for some bubbly at one of Nigella's book launches, and poured it directly into his feeding tube, John quickly scribbled, 'Now that's what I call a Maître d'.'

Like most of us who wake up after the night before, head in hands at the memory of last night's ramblings, John would thumb through his notebooks and blanch. Victoria Coren said that tabloid editors would have killed to get hold of the gossip scribbled there, but that most of it was the usual drunken nonsense. She remembers him with one particularly bad hangover wondering why he would have written, 'My parents bought him an alabaster hunchback in 1968.'

This was a time of recklessness and living in the moment, new Harleys to replace those stolen when they had lived in Notting Hill, and gambling with Charles Saatchi and his network of media chiefs. Charles was much more reclusive in character, and would not have felt comfortable holding court at many of the media parties that were Diamond's recreation of choice. But their friendship, carved over a weekly game of Scrabble upstairs at Montpeliano restaurant in Knightsbridge, was real. 'Charles makes people feel at ease because he's so at ease with himself,' Nigella has said of him. They shared the game with Carlton TV chairman Michael Green and BBC boss Alan Yentob.

For John, this was the next and final step on the network ladder. How his parents must have *kvelled*; this boy from Stoke Newington had reached the giddy heights of the media when he had nothing more to gain, when the most powerful men in the media and arts sought out a wit so sharp and a charisma so enchanting that he didn't even need a tongue to share it.

I asked one of his colleagues on the *Sunday Times* what,

apart from *chutzpah*, it would have taken the arch networker to leap from the Groucho Club to the Montpeliano. 'I would have thought it was a question of whether you could stay awake long enough,' he laughed. He said that the Saatchis and Yentobs of this world would have been as charmed as anyone else would have been by John's 'amazing gift of the gab. He was very talented. He was a very clever writer and he would turn his hand to anything. He could turn out top notch copy in an instant. And he could talk. John was always going to be good. Yentob and Saatchi would have sought him out like we all did.'

The games they played were not just a test of spelling skill and verbal pomposity. Money would change hands – as much as £5,000 in an afternoon, according to some sources. And it was after one of these hedonistic afternoons that John brought Saatchi home to meet the family. The chaotic Bohemian atmosphere of Goldhawk Road was a tonic for Charles, and he quickly became a regular visitor. While he and John indulged their Scrabble habit, his daughter Phoebe would play with Cosima and Bruno, and Nigella would cook. Perhaps Charles was even the inspiration for the Billionaire's Shortbread recipe Nigella wrote for the Gold Issue of *Vogue* in December 2000.

Victoria Coren introduced John to her favourite casino. 'It was a fairly low-rent basement joint, certainly not one of those top-drawer Mayfair places, but John wasn't fussy. My God, those other gamblers (gloomy addicts in trouble and cheap tweed) would stare when Diamond came in, usually with two or three glamorous blonde friends and a TV star or two, to chuckle over a game of casino stud. Nigella was indulgent about John's foolish hobby, happily leaving him to it; but occasionally she too came along, looking just like Claudia Cardinale in black velvet trousers. John gazed proudly across as she placed her bets, and for a moment you'd swear you were in a beautiful black-and-white 1950s film, not a smoke-filled, garishly carpeted West London basement full of slot machines.'

Victoria's account of the dying days is more upbeat than perhaps some other friends remember. 'I haven't been in many homes of the terminally ill,' she wrote in the *Observer*, 'but it must be rare to find one so glowingly warm and happy, buzzing with fun and games, with children skipping about in fancy dress, grown-ups betting on Scrabble. Every day felt like Christmas Day; it was somewhere you always wanted to be. The title of Nigella's next book, *How to be a Domestic Goddess*, was supposed to be an ironic one, but, John said: "It isn't ironic to me." '

Between caring for her dying husband, bringing up two children, making another series of *Nigella Bites* and writing the book of the series, she, like John, continued her weekly newspaper columns. John regaled his readers with stories about the effect his continuing to smoke had on those around him, while Nigella was busy pontificating about designer kitchen equipment for *Vogue* (according to Nigella we all need a Haussler Electric Bread Oven, a Woll Fish Pan, a Waring Juicer, a Robot Coupe Ice Cream Maker and an Outdoor Chef Gas Barbecue, not to mention the suede potholders from Dean and De Luca and the silver Marmite lid from Theo Fennell at £90 including Marmite). Then she moved on to foot maintenance and body creams in her make-up column in *The Times*. 'The cream that smells best to me, should you want to know,' she wrote, 'is Chanel Coco Creme Pour Le Corps (£50, from major department stores) ... I tend to bathe at night, so I want a cream that isn't fitted with a fragrance intended to make you feel too brisk.' What else were they going to do with their lives? Sit around and wait for death? Life, Nigella would say, goes on.

Besides, what better way to take your mind off things than get paid to be pampered? The trouble is that it was becoming compulsive. 'This has been a corrupting business,' she wrote in the summer before John died. 'I started as someone who was the smug epitome of low-maintenance woman: a facial once a year, if that, and not much more often at the hairdresser's. Now – unless I take myself in hand – I'm in danger of becoming a treatment junkie. I feel life is severely compromised if I don't have my eyebrows sculpted by Vaishaly Patel regularly; I dream of Eve (Lom: but then, I think I always did). I seriously have thoughts – if thought is really an appropriate word in these circumstances – like "I really must have a facial." What kind of monster are you turning me into?'

Perhaps because she was determined to play out her role as TV cookery queen of the moment for as long as she could, or because she needed to take her mind off the reality of her life, Nigella wrote another food book in 2000. The title, suggested by John, would assure her place in the public consciousness, even among those who would never set eyes on her TV persona. *How to be a Domestic Goddess,* Nigella explained in the introduction, is a book about baking. Written at a time when comfort food was an essential part of her life, it was, she said, about 'the familial warmth of the kitchen we fondly imagine used to exist ... a way of reclaiming our lost Eden'. It's about dispensing with the efficacy of cooking and indulging in sugar, chocolate, ground almonds, Frangelico even – a sigh of relief on the supermarket run and a chance to wallow in the prospect of doing something really self-indulgent. Few people, apart perhaps from parents of small children, manage to bake in the afternoon. And probably just as few will prepare a dessert for a dinner party after getting home from work and putting the kids to bed, preferring a gorgeous tart from the patisserie down the road with a spoonful of marscapone on the side. According to Nigella, however, we owe it to ourselves to bake.

CHAPTER TEN

The domestic goddess

At first, the media were with her. The launch of *How to be a Domestic Goddess* was held at what would become Goldhawk Road's second-finest kitchen and what BBC honchos now call a 'little Grouchos', the Bush Bar and Grill. A couple of doors away from Nigella's home and location for *Nigella Bites*, this was not just a venue picked so the baby monitor was still in range. At that time it had not yet been finished, which added a super-cool, rave feel to the evening to many of the guests. The publishing world had been sharpening its talons in the fight to get on the guest list. The winners included a flutter of bookish but beautiful celebrities (Mariella Frostrup, A. A. Gill, Nicola Formby, Natascha McElhone), a brace of powerful agents, publishers and TV and magazine heavyweights (Ed Victor, Alexandra Shulman, Alan Yentob) and a rack of cookery personalities who served up enough quotes to make the *Evening Standard* shiver with excitement and brand Shepherd's Bush the new Notting Hill. The River Café's Rose Gray described it as 'quite New York, just like East Avenue around 24th', while Ed Victor's assistant, perhaps in the pay of a local estate agent, sported a T-shirt emblazoned with 'DA BUSH'.

Until now she had commanded almost divine worship among her peers, with female journalists stamping on each other's Jimmy Choos if one so much as uttered a jealous word. 'Wherever women journalists lunch together,' wrote Sarah Sands, a former colleague at the *Telegraph*, and her editor at the *Evening Standard*, 'conversations lead to the media goddess. One female editor I know suggests that we have not resolved Nigella, because we are denied the impulse of *schadenfreude*, which is a vital part of the journalistic process.' *Schadenfreude*, the cackling of witches over another's misfortune, is surely as vital a part of the journalistic process as boiling bones is in creating a good stock. Her female fans love her because she's not thin and brings cookbooks back into the bedroom, and men love her because men like curvy women. What needs to be resolved?

When *How to be a Domestic Goddess* hit the desks of the food editors, the media witches became apoplectic. How could the bluestocking, Oxford-educated food writer who changed a generation's eating habits have turned into a kind of fifties housewife paraded in heart-shaped pinnies? Nigella may have intended irony in both the title and the iconography, but she was playing a dangerous game. A press backlash was inevitable, and for the queen of cookery to write a book about baking while her husband was on his deathbed was just too much. 'There may be men,' declared Melanie McDonagh in the *Evening Standard*, 'who imagine that the title of Ms Lawson's new book is pleasingly, self-deprecatingly ironic.' Not McDonagh. 'What we're buying into here is nothing so mundane as recipes: it's the girl herself, projected on to her home and appearance, and far removed from the straitened world of the watching punters. All that's needed is for her to pose for *GQ* to make her into an icon of the times.'

Nigella was surprised and saddened. 'I wasn't claiming to be a domestic goddess, so I was quite surprised when people started applying it to me. I got irked by it. But I did bring it on myself,' she admits. 'Someone was saying in an article about me that I was betraying the sisterhood by going back to the kitchen. I can't blame them because I know if I was writing an article about my book I'd have picked on that, too. But you can't take these things too seriously and focus on other people's reaction. It'd be too easy to get self-absorbed … In the introduction [to *Domestic Goddess*] I say that I have no desire to confine anyone to the kitchen quarters. And when I talk about the "familial warmth of the kitchen we fondly imagine used to exist", I think I make it clear that I don't believe it ever did. So the charitable view is to say that the book has been wilfully misunderstood to make good copy, because I think otherwise one is saying that the level of dimness is quite staggering. So why should I mind that? What did Liberace say? "I cried all the way to the bank." '

'How long will it last?' was the big question. It wasn't just her book sales, but the era of the domestic goddess 'who effortlessly juggles a full-time career with babies, household chores and cordon bleu cooking' that was said to be over. 'According to a new survey,' said the *Daily Telegraph*, 'nine out of ten working women are worn out and stressed by the relentless pressures of work and home. Given the option, only a fifth would choose to be a "career woman".' Cherie Blair,

Victoria Beckham, Carol Vorderman and Nigella Lawson were among the worst offenders, and 94 per cent of women surveyed said they were irritated by the celebrity 'can do it all' female. It probably didn't help that she'd just been voted Third Most Beautiful Woman in the World. Articles like Lucy Mangan's 'Who's Afraid of Nigella Lawson?' appeared in the *Guardian*, with Lucy playing the role of innocent surrounded by an army of Nigella/Jamie/Delia-trained uber-cooks doing things with butter that shouldn't be allowed. 'I possess none of Nigella's oeuvre,' wrote Mangan defensively, 'for much the same reason that I don't own any floor-length pictures of Elle Macpherson or set fire to myself on a regular basis.'

Once the knives were out, she was anyone's game, and soon questions were asked about the source of her recipes. 'Hot on the heels of the shocking revelations about Nigella Lawson's recipe for chocolate orange cake,' gasped the *Evening Standard*, 'I am told that the recipe is not even her own.' It turns out the cake has had many lives, appearing first in *The Great Book of Desserts* by Maida Heatter, published in America in 1974, and again in *The Cake Bible* by Rose Levy Beranbaum. 'Nigella has been rumbled before using other people's recipes for her television show. I reported in April 2002 that she paid Trinny "You-Are-What-You-Wear" Woodall's personal chef, Skye Gyngell, £2,000 for ten of the recipes she used in the hit series, *Nigella Bites*.'

Nigella had always been clear that, for her, cooking is about loving food, remembering snippets of information from kitchens you've loved – either made of shiny steel and located in New York and London, or of old wood and burnt pots in family homes of your youth. There are very few completely new ideas – Heston Blumenthal and El Bulli aside – and Nigella doesn't claim to offer anything more than recipes evolved from those she's discovered in bedtime reads and ideas shared over a bottle of wine ('I've acquired an unfortunate taste for expensive reds, which don't give me a headache,' she told *Sainsbury's* magazine). 'There just aren't any new recipes,' she told the Royal Society of Literature. 'People and ingredients have been around for a very long time. If they haven't been put together before, it's probably for a very good reason.'

Of course, not crediting recipes is just not kosher. And Nigella agrees. 'You should always credit where you found a recipe even if you change it slightly. Just because it's interesting to know where it's from. I'm always finding people who have taken my recipes and not acknowledged it.' And in her defense, she does seem to be meticulous, quoting her assistant's sister's mother-in-law for a Christmas cake in *Feast*.

American food columnist and author Barbara Kafka says that she used one of her recipes. 'I forget which one, but she asked me for permission, and she was very nice about it.' American food editor Susan Spungen was rather flattered when she spotted an idea she had used in *Martha Stewart Living* magazine extremely similar to one Nigella had included in *Domestic Goddess*. 'In a sense, that's what people like Martha and Nigella do – they distil what's going on out there for the rest of us. I saw a picture of her surrounded by recipe books as if it was a reference to where she gets her inspiration from, and I thought, "Yes, that's what she does." '

According to some critics, Nigella was beginning to believe her own hype. 'What was lovely about her at the beginning was that she would say things like, "I'm not a real expert," said Janice Gabriel. 'The further she went, the less produced she was in the end,' she said. 'They'd created a character. She couldn't talk food in terms of sourcing or measurements, and that's probably why she developed that role at first. Suddenly they'd be late starting the shoot because her hair wasn't right and her make-up wasn't right – this wasn't long before John died. And there was quite a lot of talk about getting things ready. Apparently there was even a discussion on botox in the last series. And you thought, God, she really doesn't need this. She is so gorgeous.' Television is a demanding child of a medium, a monster that can dominate the lives who fall into its thrall, but piling the weight on its victims, calling them all times of the day and night and deliberately misinterpreting their words. It takes a wise person to allow it to play its tricks without taking it personally, but even Nigella who prides herself on her slatternly approach to make up and image, succumbed to television's demand for her to have her hair cut. 'If you're standing over a pan of steaming water for hours, it has to be fixed,' said Nigella pragmatically. 'Plus, being so bosomy means that I have to have the microphone in my hair, not down my bra. You get noises known as "bra creep" in the business. So the mic is on the top of my head and I have to have my hair quite bouffant to hide it.'

Having always done her own make up until now, an expert was called in. Nigella scribbled her own top tips in her very last make-up column in *The Times* in December 2001. The Nefertiti image can be created thus; 'As far as I'm concerned, a slash of Black Smoke (applied by dipping an eyeliner brush in Paula Dorf's Transformer as eyeliner, with a smudge of Temptation (a vaguely glittering mid-brown) or Paris by

Night (a deeper brown) applied with an angled eye contour brush along the socket and blended with the Mac brush no. 216 is all the eye-enhancement you will ever need – along with a quick press with Paula Dorf's eyelash curlers and a brush of mascara.' She found plenty of new mascaras to play with but always returned to her favourite, the Agnes B lash-building mascara in black.

She is the Imelda Marcos of the lipstick world, with more shades of beigey nudes than any girl could reasonably make use of. In fact, more than she could reasonably make use of either. 'I have about 36 of them' she wrote, 'but mostly I wear none of them, in favor of a quick slick of Ultima II's volumising lip balm.'

Watching her latest daytime ITV show, *Nigella* in which she seems to take great glee in rummaging through handbags and comparing girly goods with her guests, we get an inkling of how she must have loved opening those jiffy bags stuffed with make up. 'I can't find better face or blusher brushes than Versace,' she wrote. 'I prime that face with Estee Lauder's Idealist, which fills in lines and plumps up tired complexions and if the situation is urgent, I resort to a bed-time application of Estee Lauder's Night Repair serum'. She signed off with her characteristic 'have-a-go' attitude, giving us the idea that beauty is about more than a posh lip brush. 'Taste is subjective, of course, but I have never pretended to be anything but subjective. Still – and as a note to end on, it has I hope a wider application – enthusiasm rather than expertise is what gets us through life.'

It wasn't just her lashes that were to be teased for the show. Carmen rollers and a superstar snipper, John Barrett, the celebrity photographer who spun Liza Minelli's hair with such dexterity for her wedding that she even left behind the tiara she'd planned on wearing, were brought in for the occasion. Before Barrett was allowed to cut the length, her curtain of hair would act as a rather useful hiding place from the world, but Barrett spotted something in her that was bursting to get out. 'I shaped her hair round her face to bring out her allure, to let the vamp out,' he said. 'I'd always had long hair,' explained Nigella, 'down to my waist at one point, and I had a phobia about going to the hairdresser. John (Barrett) was the first person to cut some length off my hair without my minding. He gave me a style. He also introduced me to groomed eyebrows to which I'm now addicted. But if the face had now been revealed and a new confidence born, the coiffing was short lived outside her kitchen studio. 'I'm not really a groomed type,' she said. 'I would like to be high maintenance, but I haven't got what it takes. I've never told John, but sometimes my assistant Hettie trims my hair with the kitchen scissors.' Apparently the only time that Nigella used a styling brush, it got stuck in her hair.

Flirting with the camera and playing dress-up in the world she and her crew had created in the basement of her Goldhawk Road home, *Nigella Bites* was more than just a cookery program for her. And Flashback was becoming more than just another new production company; it was this team that stood beside her as her life took its next dramatic turn.

CHAPTER ELEVEN

We have made us who we are

After four years of illness, with the cancer spreading to his lungs and the increasing realization that the end was in sight, John began to pull away from his family and the people around him. Nigella believes that it was the only way he could bear to leave them. 'I think that in order for people to die when they are young, they have to detach themselves from life, otherwise it's too painful for them,' she told Lynda Lee-Potter. 'I'm sure he felt calm about me because there was nothing unfinished about our relationship. But leaving Cosima and Bruno was a terrible thing because that was unfinished business. They were going to grow up and change and he wouldn't be there. We didn't talk too much about them because leaving them was too awful for him to contemplate.'

That she was filming by day, presenting herself as a domestic goddess and inspiring her fans with her matter-of-fact yet hedonistic attitude to life, while John was slipping away, is astonishing. 'I'd give Bruno his night feed and go to the hospital. Then I'd leave very early in the morning so the children wouldn't know I'd been away.' Working took her mind off the everyday reality and the tiredness that inevitably followed her long nights with John at the Royal Marsden. 'I cook for fairly selfish reasons,' she told Andrew Billen in the *Evening Standard* six months before John died. 'I find it restful. I'm someone who lives too much in her own head, and I find the repetitive actions calming like something someone else might do in a gym. Occasionally it goes overboard and I tend towards neurotic compulsion, doing too much when I am really tired.'

Cooking for her was symbolic of how she was dealing with the rest of her life. 'It's about allowing yourself to feel part of the chaos in a safe way, because cooking isn't a precise art. There's a science that dictates what happens to certain ingredients at certain temperatures, but nevertheless you can't have absolute control over the outcome. You have enough control to be interested, but you're allowing yourself to dabble in the chaos, dip your foot into it without feeling there's a risk of drowning in it.'

Home life was up and down but, in spite of everything, Nigella's and John's strong resolve to keep the children's lives as normal as possible seemed to be paying off. 'They are happy children, and John's wonderful with them,' she said in October 2000. 'He's much better than I am with them because he's more playful and funnier, and also stricter.' She promised to herself that she would never lie to them about John, and if they asked, as they invariably did, a searingly honest question such as 'Is Daddy going to die?' she had her answer. 'I'd say, "Yes, he could die, but the doctors are doing all they can to make him better." ' But they were always aware, as kids are, of everything that went on. 'If John is due to go into hospital for some tests, the children will wake up in the middle of the night because they can sense the anxiety,' she said.

In the week before he died John appeared to give up. He had told a friend that he didn't want to 'do this' any longer and, terrifyingly, on 28 February 2001 he began to hemorrhage at home. Luckily the children weren't there at the time, and he was rushed to hospital, where it happened again. 'That's it now,' wrote John in a note to Nigella. 'Don't do anything to keep me going. I've had enough,' adding in another note, 'Kiss the children for me.'

Nigella and a few close friends stayed with him until, two days later, he asked the doctors to 'take me under and relieve the pain and waiting. Please.' He underlined the word 'please' twice. 'Stay with me is all,' he scribbled to Nigella, according to one of the friends who visited. 'As long as the last is with you, that's OK.'

There was no time to get the children to the hospital to say goodbye, and it was up to Nigella to go to their school to tell them herself. 'Telling Mimi and Bruno was the worst thing I have ever had to do in my life,' she told Lynda Lee-Potter. 'I was terrified somebody would mention something before I got there because it was on the news. I said, "Daddy was very ill and the doctors tried to make him better, but they can't." Bruno said, "I am so sad Daddy died, so sad." ' He was four years old.

'I sometimes feel this huge disconnection between how things are perceived and how things were,' Nigella told Louette Harding in May 2001, two months after John's death. She says she didn't really believe that he was dying, that his column was about being professionally terminally ill. 'I somehow thought that he'd carry on being like that for ever.'

The funeral was a Jewish one, and Olivia Lichtenstein said she got an inkling of what she (and her siblings) must have been like at school when the rabbi came over to discuss the funeral that John had requested at the Liberal Jewish Synagogue in North London. 'As he entered the kitchen,' she writes in *Eve*, 'I tried to shield the pork sausages on the table from his view with my body. We were all in a fairly distressed state and his opinions on the service never really stood a chance among this gathering of journalists and editors. His proposed service was, I'm afraid, slashed to pieces. And as he spoke to us, I had a clear idea of the insubordination of the Lawson siblings. Horatia stifled insolent giggles and Dominic did what Nigella calls his "rolling eyes and falling timber". (To achieve this, roll your eyes irritably headwards and allow your body to lean dangerously to the side as if about to fall out of your chair.) Nigella was scarily aloof: "I'm not very good at authority," she says.'

According to Christopher Silvester, who was one of the mourners, in true Diamond fashion the funeral was 'fantastically well attended'. Charles Elton, one of John's best friends, and Dominic Lawson were among those who read the addresses. 'John's way of dealing with it wasn't quite as funny in real life as it was in the columns,' Dominic reminded the friends who had watched the rages and the despair, the venison stew being thrown across the kitchen floor when his lack of tongue made it impossible to swallow the tiniest morsel of it, and Nigella's endless self-control in the face of it.

'There was a very, very deep anger which didn't always come out in his writing. I think this was a huge burden for him and a huge burden for Nigella.'

Nigella read his last words, recorded in his trusty notebook, to the many mourners: 'How proud I am of you and what you have become. The great thing about us is that we have made us who we are. Kiss the children for me. I love you all.'

It was, of course, tremendously moving, and even that most cynical of tribes, the journalists, found it almost too much to bear. Christopher Silvester, someone who is not given to extravagant displays of emotion, broke down in tears. 'There was this very long slow queue to offer their condolences to Nigella and Dominic and John's family, and I remember I could feel a surge of emotion building up. It was almost like when you're going to be sick. I managed to control it until the moment when I was shaking hands with Dominic and I turned to Nigella, then I completely lost it, which is quite rare for me. She was very good about it. She did the classic Jewish-mother thing and comforted me. Then I went out into the area outside and was comforted by Adrian [A. A.] Gill, who was almost as motherly as Nigella – hard to imagine, I know. And Rosie Boycott comforted me as well. I was just feeling how awful it was for Nigella and the children, and I was feeling the loss of John, but there was also a slight sense of guilt that I hadn't seen enough of him in the past eighteen months. As I recall it, there were a couple of stages when it looked quite hopeful that he was going to beat the cancer – though he hated talking about it in terms of a battle.'

For John's readers, there was suddenly a terrible silence in *The Times*. He had filed his copy, as had Nigella, through the most extraordinary of circumstances, although on one occasion when John had undergone one of many operations he asked her why her witty, breezy column hadn't appeared that week. She reminded him that she had been with him, nursing him back to consciousness. Such details almost never stopped him fulfilling his own obligations.

John's columns gave him a chance to put down for posterity what glimpses of light he might have caught in between the inevitable rants that are part and parcel of terminal illness. Many people about to die appear to reach a state of enlightenment, the moment when it all clicks into place, when the meaning of life is as clear as day.

John too, only months before his death, seemed to have found the answer, even though at home, his rage was still very real. 'This is what it's all about' he wrote in his column in *The Observer*. 'It's about reading a paper on a Sunday morning while you're thinking about whether you can be arsed to go to the neighbors' New Year's Eve party tonight. It's about getting angry with me for having different opinions from yours or not expressing the ones you have as well as you would have expressed them. It's about the breakfast you've just had and the dinner you're going to have. It's about the random acts of kindness which still, magically, preponderate over acts of incivility or nastiness'. Life, he said was about rereading all the books you've always meant to read, and betting on the horses because no-one's going to stop you. The freedom to watch old episodes of *Frasier* on satellite TV, having the choice of 'three dozen breakfast cereals and seven brands of virgin olive oil at Sainsbury's', he said is what life is really all about. But most of all, he wrote, 'It's about loving and being loved, about doing the right thing, about one day being missed when we're gone'.

Happiness, he finally discovered, was about being alive. No more, no less. And in an encapsulation of Buddhist thought, he advised his readers to enjoy being here, right now. While they still could.

'It is, above all I suppose, about passing time,' he wrote, forgetting for a moment his signature cynicism. 'And the only thing I know that you don't is that time passes at the same rate and in much the same way whether you're going to live to 48 or 148'.

The idea that the death bed is a place of peace is not always shared by those left behind, and Nigella has said that this enlightenment that was the gift he gave her during their life together was stolen from him by the cancer. 'Life was the biggest present anyone could give him,' she said. 'He was so thrilled – he couldn't believe his luck – about his work, marrying me. That's quite rare, and I found it liberating. His great tragedy is that he lost that attitude. Life became a punishment rather than a present'.

John's friend, former boss at the *Mirror* and champion, Roy Greenslade, remembers him as a sparkling wit, and a sparkling human being with an acute intelligence 'laced with gentle satire and delivered with self-deprecating charm'. He wrote about his ability to turn the worst moments into some of the most memorable. Nigella had come to visit John in the hospital after the operation which would remove any possibility of his speaking again. She whispered her greeting and with a grave expression he scribbled her a message. 'Her heart sank when she read the opening words and then, in a moment, her frown disappeared as she broke into hysterical laughter. "Before I die," he had written, "I would like you to list all the men you've ever slept with." '

Victoria Coren wrote an obituary in the *Observer*.

You always saw him first in a crowd, his blaze of blond hair and dandy suits picking him out like a lighthouse in fog; a cluster of people roaring with laughter as John scribbled jokes and observations on a pocket pad faster and more engagingly than anyone else could speak. He laughed a lot, for a dying man: he laughed a lot for any man. He moved in a crackle of energy and wit. If you or I could take only liquids, through a syringe into a stomach tube, we would huddle self-pityingly at home. For John, the only question was how to get champagne down the tube without losing the fizz?

He never lost interest in other people, however trivial our traumas seemed compared to his. Even as he lay in a lead-lined room last autumn, blasted for a solid week with radiation so strong that no visitor was allowed to stay longer than 15 minutes, he wanted to spend those 15 minutes hearing about your problems. He managed to blend an incredible amount of kindness and love for his friends with a staggering forthrightness towards those he didn't like. With months to live, John wasn't going to waste any time; if he thought someone was a bad man, he'd tell them straight. And 'bad man' is not the phrase he'd use. People who had mistreated his friends, or voiced an inexcusable opinion, would look down at that notebook and blanch. Social cowards among us looked on, and wished we dared do the same.

But with the help of Nigella, Cosima and Bruno, he had a quite incredible capacity for finding joy along the way. When you looked at him, you didn't see sadness – you saw color and light, dazzle and spirit, charm and laughter. He just shone. When John walked into a room it was like Pleasantville; the monochrome would give way to a ripple of blues and greens, pinks and golds. Without him, it's just grey.*

She quoted Tennyson to illustrate her vision of a world without him:

> He is not here; but far away
> The noise of life begins again,
> And ghastly through the drizzling rain
> On the bald street breaks the blank day.

She concluded with a thought about what her subject might have said about such an obituary. 'John would say: "The piece is fine, Toria. Just don't put that bloody maudlin quote on the end." '

Victoria emailed me to say: 'Nigella is a wonderful woman, super-bright yet sweet and loving, and she never lost that – it's so great that she has Charles to love now. I hope you are

---

* Reproduced with kind permission of Victoria Coren.

able to capture her spirit. And John, of course, was one of the most terrific people who ever existed.'

CHAPTER TWELVE

Moving on up

Fortune favors the brave, although Nigella and John denied that they did anything more noble than putting up with it and getting on in the best way they could. 'I despise the set of warlike metaphors that so many apply to cancer,' John wrote in his column. 'My antipathy has nothing to do with pacifism and everything to do with a hatred for the sort of morality which said that only those who fight hard against their cancer survive it or deserve to survive it – the corollary being that those who lose the fight deserved to do so.'

Nigella's gift was to remind us that life goes on – at least for those who are left behind. If time doesn't heal as quickly as you hope it will, then at least you can look forward to a time when it will. She wasn't sentimental or spiritual. 'I am not someone who believes that life is sacred, but I know that it is very precious,' she wrote later in *Feast*. She was arguing that food is a 'vital reminder that life goes on, that living is important ...Too much emphasis, I think, can be placed on the spiritual aspect, and the urgent need to believe that the soul of the person lives on. That oft-quoted funereal platitude about the deceased not being gone, but merely "in the next room" can feel like a painful denial of what a bereaved person is feeling. Memories are great, sure, but not yet. It takes time even to begin to accept someone becoming part of a memory bank rather than a living, breathing person; the immediate loss is entirely, shockingly physical, the feel of them. They are not in the next room. They are gone.'

'When someone dies, everyone is comforted by platitudes and "memories" because they're frightened by the ugly rawness of the pain,' she told Andrew Duncan. 'Memory is better than no memory, but sometimes you want obliteration because what you actually need, overwhelmingly to the point of mania, is their physical presence. I'll be grateful when I remember John well, rather than ill. To the outside world he went from being 100 per cent there, to 100 per cent not. It wasn't like that for me. The last months, years, were very difficult. He was scarcely here in a sense.'

She immersed herself in her work, and in retrospect she may have felt that it was too soon, but if the job of a TV personality is to show the rest of us what's possible when the world is ripped from beneath your feet, then Nigella did it with the kind of elegance that we'd expect of a domestic goddess. She comforted the children as best she could ('Any parent wants to protect their children from unhappiness, and not to be able to do that is terrible'), and lavished praise on their ability to make sense of a situation too horrible to bear. 'They coped amazingly,' she told us through the press a few months after John's death. Five-year-old Bruno was watching her unpack some groceries in the kitchen just after John died and told her, 'You know, I'm so sad that daddy has died,' and then when he caught sight of a familiar packet emerging from the shopping bags, he said in the same breath, 'Oooh, Twiglets.' 'They're so honest,' she said. 'When they're sad, they're sad, and when they're not, they're not. I'm bowled over by how they are.'

She was angry, depressed and as empty as anyone whose world has been ripped apart. But only for a while. 'It's made me stony-hearted about a lot,' she said after John died. 'If someone said, "What a tragedy, this person died, aged 82," I want to put a stiletto in their eyes. I rage and have horrible, unforgiving thoughts. I've learned to say, "This is what life is," not what you wish it was. How much nicer to be thought-less and optimistic. The luxury of idiocy. Seeing people die young has made me realize you don't spend time moping. Some see me as a tragic heroine, and that's what makes me acceptable to them. The idea I might be happy is unforgivable. Well, I'm sorry. It's better to be happy. Finish the champagne, and I'll read the children a nice story.'

Conscious thoughtlessness is far removed from the luxury of idiocy. It's about living in the moment, and for many it's the holy grail, the art of living. In the series of *Nigella Bites* that she filmed shortly after John died, she once turned to camera, lifted her eyes from the chopping and whisking and said, 'Believe me, life is so much easier when you can take such pleasure from such little things.'

Nigella said that in the last months of John's life, and just after, the second series of *Nigella Bites* was an emotional release for her and the children. 'The crew is so wonderful with the children,' she said. 'Neville the cameraman, Francis the lighting assistant and Chris the sound man come in in the morning and make paper airplanes and snapdragons with them and play and give them attention. And of course it's male attention they need and I have needed. I'm not saying this makes everything all right, obviously, but it's important that the house is full of noise and people and activity – like it's always been.'

'*Nigella Bites* was the hardest series I've ever been involved with,' said David Edgar. 'We were working long hours, and it was also emotionally exhausting for all of us. Nigella didn't see a lot of the kids, and that upset her. We were filming in the house all this time and the kids would come home from school, have tea, but then Lisa, the nanny, would take them upstairs to do their homework. It was a very domestic environment, but she was in make-up at 6.30 every morning.' The going was tough, and became tougher after John's death. 'We were turning a program around in three days to meet Channel Four's deadlines, and because of the break we took when John died. Everyone knew that John was very ill and we were halfway through the episode of *Temple Food* when he died. Everyone was terribly involved and we knew that she needed the familiarity of the team and the distraction of the show to get her through it.' Her TV world was her comfort zone, and it was only two weeks after John died that Nigella got back to work. 'John was dying for years, so it wasn't a shock when it happened,' David explained.

Watching the tragedy of John's death unfold in the Goldhawk Road kitchen created a lasting bond between the goddess and her crew. Plans are afoot for another series in 2005/6. Their humor helped her enormously, and even contributed to her recipe books: Francis's deep fried Bounty with pineapple appears in *Nigella Bites* – and Nigella said that she even cooked it for her guests at a supper party after tuna with ginger, soy and rice vinegar and Thai seafood curry.

They even helped her with the inevitable weight fluctuation that comes with emotional roller-coasters. In the diet-driven world we live in, Nigella is like anyone else when it comes to her body. She feels fine about herself until she steps on to the scales, so, to paraphrase a Tommy Cooper joke, she doesn't step on the scales. The team's weekly weigh-in ('We all knew we'd put on weight during the series,' she said), in which Nigella would come second only to Chris, the sound man, shows just how much she trusted them, and helped to lighten the atmosphere. 'I'm greedy,' she told the *Sunday Telegraph* magazine two months after John's death, and during the resumed filming. 'I eat under stress. When you're eating, the rest of the world is tuned out. And when you tune back in, you feel guilty about having been greedy, but the rest of the world is still there, so you have to carry on eating.' She put on half a stone since filming began, claiming that food was her drug. 'It's like being at the breast,' she said. 'I do mind putting on weight because you feel quite vulnerable with a camera pointing at you.'

Her brazen ability to help herself to what she needed to get through her tragedy was beginning to raise eyebrows. She was snapped leaving London restaurants as early as March 2001, only a few weeks after John had died, with John's old gambling mate and the family's frequent house-guest over the past few years, the multi-millionaire Charles Saatchi.

The *Mail on Sunday* was the first to run the story. 'How Tragic Nigella Has Become Close to Millionaire Charles Saatchi' trumpeted the headline, referencing Mrs Merton's famous question to Debbie McGee about what had attracted her to the millionaire Paul Daniels.

Bizarre articles referring to her sitting on his lap at every social occasion were probably more to do with the fantasies of male journalists who don't realize that women of a certain weight do not *do* laps, especially in the courting stage. Peter McKay, who ran the piece in the *Mail*'s Ephraim Hardcastle column, is convinced that it's true. 'It happened at the same villa party in Italy where Saatchi insisted on brushing her teeth,' he said.

The paparazzi had a field day, describing with lascivious attention to detail how Saatchi would see Nigella into taxis and how she would wave out of the back window until he was out of sight. Columns were dedicated to Nigella's ability to bring the once-shy mogul out of himself, to the opening up of a shy flower of a man who famously used the back stairs to his office to avoid being seen by his staff. He was now openly seen at Stringfellows lapping up the entertainment and strolling down Mauritian beaches with his new love. The power of Nigella's seduction could bring even the coldest of men to the boil.

Baghdad born, Charles Saatchi had fled to Britain from Iraq with his family in 1947. His parents were Sephardic Jews and mixed only with other Jews in their North London home in Finchley where Charles and his brothers David, Maurice and Philip grew up among other Persian immigrants. 'They wouldn't even say that they were Sephardic; they were Persian,' Gloria Abramoff, BBC Nations and

Regions Editor, said. 'In the fifties and sixties when I was
growing up, Hendon Jews mixed with the Finchley Jews, but
the Finchley Jews didn't mix with the Hampstead Jews. We
were very snotty about which Jews we would talk to. Ilford
wasn't OK, but Hackney was.'

The Saatchis were comfortably off, and their work ethic
was strong; Charles's father worked in the rag trade until he
was well into his nineties. 'They were delightful people,' said
Rabbi Dunner, who knew Charles's father well as a regular
lay reader in the Maida Vale synagogue where Dunner was
rabbi. The boys all attended non-Jewish schools in an
attempt to assimilate the next generation of Saatchis.
Charles went to Christ Church in Finchley where the mix of
children was ethnically balanced, but friends of Dunner
remember him as the class ruffian. 'I know people who went
to school with him who say that he was the Ronnie Kray of
his class.'

The second born of four sons and the apple of his parents'
eyes, Charles had always been driven to get what he wanted.
At the age of twenty-seven he set up the advertising agency
Saatchi & Saatchi with his brother Maurice, and with a
series of maverick campaigns that changed the face of advertising across the world the agency became an icon for the
yuppy eighties.

It was the first advertising agency to be appointed by a
British political party to help them win an election, and their
'Labor isn't Working' campaign helped to give the UK its first
female prime minister, as well as being one of the most
memorable slogans in advertising history.

As Saatchi & Saatchi helped the Conservatives through four

consecutive terms, the world was watching. Even Boris Yeltsin, Russia's first democratically elected president, was a client. Literally pushing the boundaries, the agency was the only one to operate from behind the Berlin Wall – and *on* it as it was being dismantled. It revolutionized the Japanese car industry with its launch of Lexus on to the world market, outselling BMW after only nine months, and was behind the launch of the first British astronaut, Helen Sharman, into space. It can even claim to have been one of the powers behind the demise of apartheid in South Africa. 'We were involved in three campaigns that completely changed the political climate of South Africa,' claims the agency's press office. 'The 1983 campaign to allow non-whites into parliament; 1992's referendum on power sharing; and the country's first fully democratic election two years later. This effectively signalled the end of apartheid.'

Ivan Fallon, who was Nigella's Deputy Editor at the *Sunday Times*, wrote a biography in 1988 called *The Brothers: The Rise and Rise of Saatchi & Saatchi*. 'By 1987,' he told me, 'the agency had become the biggest in the world, and it was Charles who was driving it very hard from behind the scenes. He had grown up in North London around Jews who were now making lots of money, and he wanted to be bigger and better. His friend Michael Green was making huge amounts of money.'

In a parallel with John and Nigella, Charles was also driving Maurice who, according to Fallon, was 'very bright, very organized. Charles had considerable influence over him, and was very much the senior brother of the two. Maurice would defer to Charles on all the creative issues.'

Fallon told how the Saatchis moved from advertising to pioneering the idea of 'globalization', the notion that one company can supply every service needed for any international institution of whatever size. They bought Ted Bates, the agency that invented TV advertising, and tried to buy Hill Samuel, the merchant bankers, as well as the Midland Bank. They planned to be bigger than ICI, but according to Fallon and City experts it couldn't last. 'They were crazy and over-reached. They took over companies for the sake of it.'

Saatchi & Saatchi is now owned by the French agency Publicis, the fourth largest communications group and the second largest media agency in the world. Charles Saatchi has gone on to become one of the UK's most important art collectors, bringing greater recognition to young British artists than any museum or public institution. Largely credited for creating the London art scene of the 1990s, he spotted and funded the kind of art that exploded on to the pages of the tabloids. Damien Hirst's shark suspended in a tank of formaldehyde, Tracey Emin's shrine to all the men she'd ever slept with and Rachel Whiteread's cement-filled house fired the public imagination in a way not seen for decades.

The critics woke up as if from a long sleep. 'If Rachel could drink a couple of quarts of plaster or pour resin down her throat, wait until it sets, and then peel herself away, I have a feeling she would,' wrote the American novelist A. M. Homes. 'She shows us the unseen, the inside out, the parts that go unrecognized.' Deborah Solomon of the *New York Times* thought Saatchi brought 'an adman's eye to the practice of connoisseurship; he favors art that makes an instant impact, art that surprises you and lodges in your brain, art with kicked-up visual appeal'.

He is a controversial figure among the art crowd, accused and congratulated at the same time as being a 'human Hoover' who buys art in bulk but who manipulates the market for personal gain. Damien Hirst said, 'I grew up in a world where Charles Saatchi believed that he could affect art values with buying power. He still believes he can do that.' His exhibitions have been criticized as efforts 'to inflate the value of his holdings, the sly move of a man for whom art is mainly a speculator's game', as Deborah Solomon wrote. She found him surprisingly charming when he chose to give her a rare interview in 1999. 'Saatchi is an animated, striking man of 56 with a tangle of black hair and large, watchful eyes. He was dressed casually in a white, short-sleeve shirt and loose black pants. Sitting down to lunch, he lit up a Silk Cut cigarette ("I'll never quit," he said with cheerful defiance) and mentioned he was leaving for Italy the next morning to binge on Renaissance art. Piero della Francesca is one of his passions. Racing go-karts is another. He offered me a cigarette and when (why not?) I accepted, he smiled and said, "Oh, good, we can be weaklings together." '

She was confused by him, and as one of the very few journalists to whom he had granted an interview, she liked him. 'I had expected him to be someone else, a skulking-around-in-the-shadows type, the diffident spook of legend. But now I saw that he can be extremely charming. Taking out a small note pad, he pretended to interview me ("Tell me, how did you become an art critic?") and in general displayed a disarming mix of attentiveness, modesty and wit. Two hours into our lunch, I opened my own note pad. That's when he shut down. He appeared pained and fidgeted nervously with the sugar packets on the table. "There's nothing complicated about me," he insisted with comic futility. "There are no hidden depths. As Frank Stella used to say about Minimalism, What you see is what you see." '

Later, Deborah watched Channel Four's *The Real Saatchis: Masters of Illusion* in which his character was assassinated, and wondered whether she had been duped by the advertising guru. She decided to go with her intuitive sense that he was genuine. 'I can still see him now, standing on the street corner where we parted, awaiting the taxi, hands in his pockets. He said to me then: "Do I have a good eye? I have a good eye for me. I don't know that my collection will ever satisfy anyone. But it satisfies me." '

'I wouldn't say that Charles isn't nice,' said the former Rabbi Pini Dunner of the Saatchi Synagogue, named in memory of Charles's parents and, if not patronized, paid for by Charles. 'He's got a good heart, but he's highly intelligent and focused so he can patronize easily and make you feel like you're not his equal. He's very shy socially, so maybe that's why he's so abrupt and why he said such stupid things to people – which of course they remember.' (Christopher Silvester used to think that Nigella was slightly aloof too. 'Whenever you chatted to her she was exactly the opposite, but people often said that she was quite frosty. But then she explained the reason for it to me once. I thought she'd cut me in the street one day, but in fact she's quite short-sighted, and she wears contact lenses and sometimes can't be bothered to put them in. She admitted she often doesn't wear her glasses and that she would wander around in a quite pleasant vague haze so that she wouldn't have to see anyone or anything.')

Damien Hirst called him a 'shopaholic' because of the way he threw his money at some of the most unlikely art subjects. Tracey Emin's unmade bed (for which he paid £150,000) is now resident in his own home, and he apparently has a collection of art gathering dust in warehouses around London. A lot of it comes from the graduate shows and fringe galleries that he still shops at, scouring London in his Rolls for anything that takes his fancy. They may make him a fortune, but most don't. Charles's £70 million fortune is one of those figures which is as only as good as the open market. One of Saatchi's friends told Ross Benson, 'If he ever tried to sell it all, he would flood the market, the price would collapse and he would be lucky to walk away with £20 million.'

However, in 2005 Alan Ridings wrote in the *New York Times* that Saatchi has turned his back on the Young British Artists in favor of a return to the good old painting. 'Not only has he cleared their works from his labyrinthine Thames-side gallery in the old Greater London Council building, but last month he also sold the most emblematic work of the YBA movement – Damien Hirst's "Physical Impossibility of Death in the Mind of Someone Living" – better known as the pickled shark – to an American buyer for what press accounts said was $13 million. He paid $93,000 for it in 1992.'

'I think Saatchi is dyslexic,' said Ivan Fallon, whose son is dyslexic and whose wife has written a book about it. 'I recognize a lot of the signs. He's as bright as Maurice but he never passed an exam while Maurice got firsts, scholarships and gold medals all the way. There was a great pressure on Maurice to become an academic. Charles had a remarkably short attention span; he'd walk out of films after ten minutes. He would never meet clients. Maybe he felt he couldn't sustain an intellectual argument. He never even met Margaret Thatcher – it was Tim Bell and Maurice who worked on that campaign. He didn't work hugely hard on anything – he could do more in five minutes than anyone else could in days. He could look at one of his art pieces in a nano and take in all he wanted. You could never interview him about anything – least of all his art.'

Fallon sent his manuscript to Maurice and Charles to check that it was factually correct, and after a week or so had heard nothing. 'I rang Maurice to find out what was happening,' he said. 'Maurice told me that he was having a ferocious row with Charles, who said that the book showed him as being the junior brother, and so he was refusing to speak to him or anyone else.'

Fallon went to see him himself and they worked on the text together. Although he had known Charles since the 1970s and been out with him many times, this was the first time that he had talked to anyone about anything to do with his work.

Charles told Deborah Solomon that it wasn't he, but Margaret Thatcher, who had created the canvas on which a new generation could paint. 'She created an environment in Britain where people felt they could escape the role they had been pushed into. They no longer had to be drop-outs and failures. Students like Damien Hirst felt they could do absolutely anything.' With Saatchi largely responsible for fanning the fire of Thatcherism, and Nigel Lawson creating the yuppy culture which fed a new generation of foodies and art buyers, his Eaton Square house was soon to become one of the most influential homes in Britain.

By the time he was regularly dining with Nigella at the Ivy, Saatchi was already separated from his second wife, Kay Hartenstein, an American from Bill Clinton's home town of Little Rock. According to Nigella, neither was interested in remarrying, despite John urging her to do so as quickly as possible after his death. Charles, according to Nigella, preferred 'flirtation to cosiness', although Nigella was more upfront about her intentions: 'I'm not suited to being alone.' More Bridget Jones than Garbo, she said she couldn't sit for more than two minutes on her own without phoning someone, and she is happy now that she is never without someone around. She admits to her love of being doted on, something she learned to accept from an early abundance of unconditional love from her brother, who has always treated her like a princess. She had it in bucketloads too from John, and it was something that the multi-millionaire had plenty to give her. 'I learned that it was OK to be adored,' she told Sue Lawley on *Desert Island Discs*.

Saatchi's wife, Kay, was confused and angry at the sudden change in her circumstances. According to Geoffrey Levy in the *Daily Mail*, the Saatchis had been planning to adopt only seventeen months earlier. They had had difficulties in conceiving their daughter, Phoebe, who was born in 1994. Anyone who knows how emotionally draining five difficult years of fertility treatment would have been will have some

Nigella, author of *How to Eat*, prepares to launch her career as a TV chef, 1999.

Nigella and John Diamond with Cosima (6) and Bruno (3) at the premiere of Walt Disney's *Dinosaur* at the Odeon Leicester Square in London in 2000, five months before John died.

Nigella with Bruno (6), Cosima (9) and Phoebe Saatchi (9) at the launch of Madonna's book *The English Roses* at The Rooftop Gardens in Kensington, London in 2003.

Left to right: Horatia, Dominic, Nigella and Nigel Lawson at the launch of *Feast* at the Culford Room, Cadogan Hall, London, October 2004.

Charles Saatchi and Nigella leave Cipriani Restaurant in Mayfair, London, April 2005.

other. Of course, the Jewish boy from the E
many Jewish boys from the East End, bound
escalator of upward mobility, but even i
passion for their culture and religion, t
galleries and political influence of Saatchi's
way from Stoke Newington in the 1970s. W
sculpting Thatcher's new look in the 1980s
drama and English teacher, sharpening
toughest of critics in a London girls' sch
involved in Labor politics. By the time Cha
izing modern art and moving in the world
John was writing for the *Sunday Times* and
ensconced in the champagne socialist worl
The world of the Groucho Club was son
Saatchi would not have inhabited, although
tising haunt of the 1980s. 'I'm sure he would
more than a couple of times,' said Christopl
moved in completely different circles.' He sa
rarely to be seen at the Groucho Club these
sure that she long ago desisted from serving
ship committee. She wasn't at the twenti
party last month.'

Christopher Silvester thinks the idea tha
the high life while her husband was suffe
ridiculous. 'I don't think at any stage she co
shirking her responsibilities towards her dyi
was there for him all the time, and for the cl
ular. She really lived through that illness v
cancer sufferer's relative does. You can't esca

'There is a vast difference between how t

th
Sa
ob
th
ac
ch
It
w
h
la
tl
il
a
y

r
f
f
t
c

outside and how they feel on the inside,' Nigella told
ly Vincent. 'I have thought badly of other people,
erving the dying and the death and then the treachery of
remarriage, quick as a knee-jerk. But I keep my own
unt to myself in the sense that if John's parents and my
dren were OK about everything, and I was, then that's it.
ounds like something on a very trite T-shirt, but life is
t happens. And, yes, sometimes I think that it would
e been better to have waited, for it to have happened
r, but I didn't and it didn't, and I went along with it. I
k maybe when you live with someone who is really very
or a long time, it somehow gives you more of a greedy
etite for life and maybe, yes, you are less measured in
behavior than you would otherwise be.'

igella also refuted the idea that John had arranged the
riage in advance. 'When people die, they detach themselves
life,' she said. 'They don't sit there thinking about the
re that doesn't include them.' Christopher Silvester knew
John was concerned that Nigella should have someone to
for her and the children once he had gone, and said it
d have been in character for John to have encouraged her
e with a rich, powerful Jew. Charles Saatchi, already a
onal friend, was a perfect match. 'John was a wonderful
ination of a socialist and a shameless social climber – in
icest possible way. He loved the fact that he'd married
la Lawson from the wealthy Lawson-Salmon clan, but he
t in a jokey way and would take the piss out of it. My view
at in a situation like this the partners will negotiate
situations themselves, and it's nobody's business
heirs.'

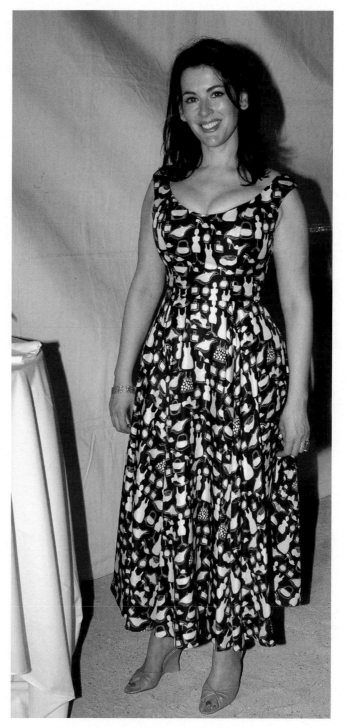

Finally a celebrity in America, Nigella is invited as a food pundit to
The South Beach Food and Wine Festival in Miami Beach, Florida,
February 2005.

During his illness, John, Nigella and Charles shared Tuscan holidays in the villa Charles rented with his wife Kay, although more often than not by this time the Saatchis were taking their holidays separately with their own friends. A friend told the *Daily Mail* that John would have been happy that Nigella got together with Charles, whom he liked enormously, after his death, as he would not have wanted her to be alone.

Nigella has said that she would have wanted John to do the same if he'd been the one left behind. Comedienne Maria McErlane was John's Charles, his 'blonde wife', as Nigella called her. 'If the position had been reversed, I'd have loved the idea of John being with Maria. I'd far rather he was with somebody I liked. It would be terrible to think of the children having a stepmother I loathed.'

The romance was heady, and the months following John's death were filled with expensive dinners, glamorous holidays and a full-on work schedule to finish the second series of *Nigella Bites*. By late August 2001, five months after John's death, rumours were even flying around that she was already pregnant after spending the summer in Tuscany with her new love. The media were beside themselves with stories of the sexy merry widow. It was the silly season for everyone, and it was only a matter of time before the inevitable fall.

CHAPTER THIRTEEN

Nigella in Wonderland

By autumn 2001 reality had caught up with Nigella, and she became deeply depressed. 'I had a complete slump,' she said. 'It was odd because I carried on completely as normal after John died. I wanted to give in to feeling terrible. I used to take the children to school and go back to bed. I couldn't work.' She did, of course, although she showed an unusual chink in her armor in her make-up column. 'There's something so hopeful about fashion,' she wrote in September 2001. 'A new season, a new look: somehow it makes us believe in change and essential, reinvigorating transformation. I should admit, though, I don't entirely subscribe to this optimistic ethos. I don't like change.' In October things were still rough: 'There's an advertising campaign running at the moment, though I can't remember for which cosmetics company (yes, that successful) to the effect that when times are really bad "there's always lipstick",' she wrote. 'Well, I can't profess that's an alien sentiment, but girls, I don't think it's really going to play right now.'

Support is usually forthcoming for the newly bereaved,

but it's what happens when the new term starts and everyone goes back to work that's really hard. And Saatchi was there, with the time, the love and the money to give her what she needed. Her children were begging her to move on and out of the family home into which John had breathed so much life, and so by the end of 2001 she found herself preparing for her first Christmas in Saatchi's £7 million terrace overlooking Eaton Square in London's Belgravia, and a new life for them all.

The criticism came, of course, although as both John and Nigella were enormously popular within the small world that is newspapers the headlines were kinder than they might have been: 'Nigella, the tycoon and why she has the right to be happy', 'Domestic Goddess moves to Heaven', 'Children pestering me to remarry', 'A sweet and sour life'. Carole Malone wrote in the *Sunday Mirror*: 'If Nigella found some comfort, good luck to her. Who are we to judge?' But, as *Private Eye* pointed out, there is one rule for journalists and quite another for the rest of the world. Malone had a different take on the relationship between Sir Paul McCartney and Heather Mills the year before: 'I suppose that having listened as Paul told us about Linda being his soul mate, the love of his life and how they'd only spent three nights apart in 30 years, I'm disappointed that just 18 months after her death he meets a beautiful blonde at a charity event and – hey presto – there's an instant attraction.'

Nigella took the rough with the smooth. 'I think it's different when someone dies over a long time from how one would respond to a sudden death. Also, in a funny way, if you have been happily married there are no unresolved areas, nothing to prove to yourself after the other dies. Statistically, people who have been happily married and then widowed tend to remarry. Those who were unhappily married tend to stay single, which kind of makes sense. And I can't say, "It's all a bit quick, I'm not going to go with it." I have to go with how I feel.'

She concentrated her energies into creating a new life for herself and the children in Belgravia. Cosima is at school now with Phoebe, a far cry from the primary school in Goldhawk Road. Nigella had been keen not to take on any debts while John was ill, but her choice of state school at the time also reflected her attitude towards private education. 'I don't want my children to go to a school where everyone's got big houses and the children have to wear felt hats,' she told Tamasin Day-Lewis in 1999. 'It's another kind of ghetto.' And Bruno is, Nigella has said, a chip off the old block. 'I think he's very clever but I don't know whether he will be academic. But then John and Charles are the cleverest men I have ever met, and have they ever passed an exam? Being driven, original, quick and clever are the things that get you through.'

With neighbors such as Sean Connery, Belgravia is a million miles away from Goldhawk Road, where the kebab bars soak up the gamblers making their way out of the local street market with exotic fish and Afro-Caribbean fruit and veg. in their carrier bags. In her new home Tracey Emin's installation of an unmade bed takes over a whole room, and a barefooted workman, apparently attending to some repair in the upstairs hall, is another work of art. There are members of staff everywhere. Nigella has her own library and her own secretary in her own company, Pabulum (described in the dictionary as 'A substance that gives nourishment; food. Insipid intellectual nourishment: "TV … gobbled up comedy material and spat it out as pabulum."') in the basement. Tattinger champagne rather than a bottle of expensive red is the afternoon's sneaky cocktail. She has kept the old house on the Goldhawk Road as the location for her cookery programs, and is landlady to her little sister, Horatia.

The Lawson connection to Shepherd's Bush is unlikely to be forgotten, not just because of the memories of her time with John and the birth of her children, but also because it was once home to the headquarters of J. Lyons and Co., Cadby Hall, which stood on the corner of Brook Green just off Hammersmith Road. Nigella has even written a fore-word to a cookbook written by pupils at the local Brackenbury primary school as a token of her love for her old manor.

The children love their new school and their new life, and never talk about going back to Shepherd's Bush. Nigella told Sue Lawley about their reaction to news of the move. 'I was saying to Mimi, "Darling, we're moving and it might be quite difficult," and she said in quite a patronizing way, "Mummy, I don't want to be rude, but Eaton Square is a lot nicer than Shepherd's Bush." She was eight then.' 'Nigella never did like Shepherd's Bush,' said Sarah Johnson, who moved into the area in the mid-nineties. 'Her house on that main road was like a goldfish bowl. Everyone in Shepherd's Bush could see who was knocking on her door.'

While Nigella was trying on her new life it was time to begin filming again, and suddenly she was back in Goldhawk

Road, surrounded by the family photos and memories of John, flirting with the camera and dangling noodles into her open mouth. It could never have worked, even if the new series, *Forever Summer*, was intended to be a symbolic end to her period of mourning, a chance to throw open the blinds and let the light back in. 'We opened it up and made it less stylized, took the dressing off the set, the soft material off the windows,' her producer David Edgar said. 'We wanted to look out this time. It was more about reality and less studio based.' Taking the crew to Suffolk beaches to make cocktails and curries while the sun set, padding around in a silk dressing gown and barbecuing spatchcock chicken in the summer rain was an idealized picture of the world, and considering how much was known about her new relationship it was rather empty. Viewers understood that she and the children had shared their TV home with the spectrum of John throughout *Nigella Bites*, but if her friend Fenella and her family could come and chop spring onions with her in *Forever Summer*, where was Charles?

Her critics in the UK had mixed opinions of *Forever Summer*, which was broadcast in the late summer of 2002. Victor Lewis-Smith was still drooling: 'Since the day the world discovered that Diamonds are not for ever,' wrote the super-sensitive critic in the *Evening Standard*, 'she's become even more pert and shapely, and her every gesture now seems marinated in erotic overtones. But surely not even Freud could explain why the phrase "duck fat" kept running through my mind as I watched her spooning chocolate sauce over a giant pineapple kebab before greedily sucking it off.' He praised *Forever Summer* as 'vastly superior' to *Nigella*

Bites. 'It's [because of] Ms Lawson's increasingly deliberate use of her sexuality, from her first sultry "hello" to her final coy "chin chin" (which as I suspect she knows is Japanese for "penis penis").'

Forever Summer, the book of the series, was a bland medley of recipes culled from books and holidays, and compared with the hugely influential *How to Eat* it was considered lightweight. After the mixed reactions to *Domestic Goddess*, the press was warming up for a serious backlash. 'She did begin to get some terribly bad press,' David Edgar said. 'I remember sitting with Nigella and Michael Jackson, who was the chief executive of Channel Four at the time, and reading through some of them. There's not a person on Earth who could stand that kind of criticism. Mostly people were still enjoying what we were doing, and we were enjoying doing it, but in this business criticism of your work and the way you work is crucial to your confidence. People who present have a certain kind of ego – it motivates you to want to perform, and criticism can fatally undermine you. But she didn't show that she was upset. She wouldn't have revealed how she felt about it.'

The final straw came when she was doing a photo shoot, and she confided to a journalist that Charles Saatchi found her sexier than Marilyn Monroe. The result was a backbiting article that turned up the heat; Nigella said it was no fun walking the kids to school that morning. She responded by telling the *Guardian*, 'What happened was he called me over and said, "Marilyn Monroe's belly sticks out, so why do you moan about yours?" If being misquoted is the worst thing that happens to me this year, then I shall count myself blessed. The news story transferred something from my husband to me. You can't comment on something you didn't say. "Husband is nice to wife" is not a news story.'

But she was upset at what she saw as the press's malevolence. 'They set you up, make the image that they want and then blame you for it. I'll never do it again,' she said, referring to that comradely whisper to a fellow journalist. 'From now on I must take full responsibility for what I agree to do.'

She now launched a publicity campaign of her own, talking only to a select group of journalists. 'I thought, I'm so tired,' she told one of her chosen journalists. 'Why am I doing this? I'm frightened of a break because no one knows what will happen. I might give up earning my living from cooking at some point. I've never planned my life.' In a string of interviews she seemed to be writing the obituary of the Domestic Goddess, and reclaiming her personal life. She told her friend Olivia Lichtenstein in *Eve* magazine back in 2002, 'I don't inhabit a celebrity world, and I don't lead a première lifestyle. I have my friends who know me. I used to be oversensitive, but now I keep a distance between myself and what's said about me. I don't need to be recognized. I'm not an actress and I can only be me.'

But even her viewers were giving up on her. *Forever Summer* was a flop, peaking at under a million viewers in the UK. '*Forever Summer* was just a continuation of *Nigella Bites*,' said David Edgar. 'Some of it was the best she ever did. We moved it on, but there was a fatigue around food shows. We were all exhausted. We'd peaked. Remember that Nigella had come into TV cookery quite late on, and TV was already shifting towards reality shows. Nigella was left hanging out to dry. Channel Four didn't quite know what to do with her. They felt that with *Forever Summer* her time had come to an end.'

Nigella had always been protected by her brother, by John, by the network of rich and powerful friends around her, and now she was confused. 'I think she felt a degree of surprise that she wasn't more supported by Channel Four,' said her former producer. 'They went very quiet at the time.' However, a series of factors might have contributed to the failure of *Forever Summer*. For one thing, the scheduling wasn't good. 'I think the first episode went out in the late summer of 2002 when all her constituency would still be on their holidays in Tuscany.' And remember that her appeal wasn't universal. 'We knew that there would be a press backlash sooner or later; we just didn't know when it would come. After she had moved in with Charles, we suspected it would come soon. Our world is dominated by the media rather than the public. It's the media that set the agenda, and they had decided that they'd had enough of Nigella. We felt that we were working towards complete exhaustion in TV. The press are a bit like the City of London and work on the boom or bust. They build you up and then knock you down.'

Although her crew were discussing a new cookery series with her in 2005, Janice Gabriel believes that the Nigella phenomenon has come to the end of its life. 'It got difficult to make at the end; she kind of ran out of ideas. And if you look at the books, they're pretty much all from *How to Eat*. It didn't really evolve foodwise. And the reason for that was that she'd pretty much written the book for the lifestyle that she had. She didn't want to change that. She didn't want to become a chef.'

If she was surprised at the lack of support from the powers that be at Channel Four, at least Nigella knew that popular culture is a fickle beast. 'I have no desire to be a fashionable person,' Nigella had prophetically told the *Observer*'s Harriet Lane back in 2000 when she was facing the prospect of being a single mother of two. 'That means that you'll go out of fashion. I'd rather be hanging around for a long time. My son is four; I can't afford to be unemployed in a few years' time. I was frightened that the program might be constraining, that I'd be turned into just a food person. But in a way it's my job not to let that happen.' When it did, it hurt. As she told Sue Lawley, she is sensitive – 'the definition of sensitive being vain and touchy', she said. 'I am also highly strung and a bit of a nightmare. But for some reason – maybe it's with Jorgie [her nickname for Charles] – I seem to have developed a sense of proportion. Not always. If someone is trying to be wounding, the chances are that they will succeed and they will wound. But I don't think I let it define what I think I am.'

Her life was becoming more settled outside of the flighty world of TV, and it felt right to make it even more solid. The children wanted her to remarry. 'Children are very conservative, aren't they?' she said before she finally succumbed to Saatchi's charm. 'They believe in marriage, which is great, but it's also because of their egotism. Children see everything according to how it impinges on them. They think it would be exciting for them, but they're not old enough to have firm views. I can understand, though, that they like the idea of stability.' Children also take things very seriously, and John's request that they 'make sure that Mummy remarries' would probably have been a burning mission for them. Imagine the high fives behind their closed bedroom door after Nigella broke the news to them that she was to become the next Mrs Saatchi.

CHAPTER FOURTEEN

The domestic Jewess

Charles asked Rabbi Pini Dunner to perform the marriage service with only one other person in attendance, something which under Jewish law is not allowed. Not only would Rabbi Dunner have to persuade him to find the ten Jewish men necessary, but he would also have to authenticate Nigella's Jewish status. 'There were a lot of the Salmon family who had married out,' Dunner said, 'and I just couldn't be 100 per cent sure. I spent a lot of time looking into it, researching documents and graveyards, but by the time I could confirm her Jewishness they'd done it anyway.'

They married in August 2003, twenty months after she moved into his Belgravia home, with the minimum of fuss and a small family gathering to mark the occasion. But why did Saatchi, the non-practising Jew who had been married twice before to the blondest of American *shiksas*, suddenly feel the need for a rabbi? 'When I was talking to Charles about the marriage,' Dunner said, 'he was saying that recent events in the Middle East had made him feel more Jewish than ever before. Of course he might have been saying that to persuade me to marry him.'

The Saatchi brothers, including David and Philip, who book-end Charles and Maurice in age, each have a different sense of their Jewish identity. 'David lives in the Hamptons in upstate New York and is the one who is most interested in his Jewishness,' Rabbi Dunner said. 'He's the most comfortable with who he is. But he's lived in America for a while and it's very different over there. Jews don't feel that they have anything to hide there. The youngest is Philip. I think he's something in the music industry. And Maurice is married to a non-Jewish writer. She's a lovely girl. He was married to a Jewish woman first though,' he added. He said that the Saatchi parents became interested in establishing the Saatchi Synagogue when they realized they were unlikely to have any Jewish grandchildren. The Jewish religion passes through the maternal line, and Kay Hartenstein is not Jewish, nor is Phoebe. 'It was the legacy that they could leave behind,' said Dunner. 'The name would at least carry on in the community.' In the most recent of a long series of ironies in Nigella's life, this unlikely Jewess would have been able to give Charles's parents – had they survived – the only Jewish step-grand-children in the family.

The Saatchi family are not members of the Saatchi Synagogue. Charles's late parents were members of a far more orthodox congregation in Maida Vale. Rabbi Dunner is clear about the reason they used the name. 'For us at the *shul*, Saatchi Synagogue was an original name that we thought would attract a certain kind of person. We wanted to create a *cool shul*, somewhere where lots of events would take place for the kind of person who wasn't attracted to the synagogues of their youth. The Saatchi Gallery was up the road, so it seemed a great combination of words.' Deborah Solomon remembered that when the temple opened, a poster for it was plastered up throughout the London Underground – a spoof of a Damien Hirst dead-animal sculpture featuring a chicken floating in a tank of chicken soup. 'My parents think I'm nuts,' Saatchi told her.

'The *shul* was very successful for a number of years,' said Rabbi Dunner, 'although it has struggled I would say since I left in 2004. It's become more of a community synagogue where members go to meet each other, and is less of a transient community coming together in their hundreds for a really great event. It's not a bad thing, but it's different to what I set up.'

Charles and Nigella now host a weekly dinner at the Rib Room at the Carlton Tower, just around the corner from their Belgravia home. A cast that John would have been proud of joins them every Friday night: Toby Young and his Jewish wife, Caroline, Dominic Lawson and his wife, Rosa Monckton (former best friend to our late national icon, the Princess of Wales), and Rachel Johnson (Boris's sister) are among them, selected for their cultural connection rather than their little black books. If John brought out the goddess she already was, Saatchi seems to be taking the Jewess out on the town. One of the occasional cast members, a Jewish New Yorker, said that there's no significance in the dinners being held on a Friday night – the Jewish Shabbat – apart from not having to get up the next morning. When I asked him if they lit candles as part of the traditional Friday-night experience, he laughed. 'Oh my God, no. I live in the greatest Jewish city in the world and I've never seen a candle on a Friday night. If I did, I would run. It's not noteworthy in any way other than it's enormously casual and very comfortable with a great bunch of people.' He said that even Charles is relaxed. 'He's very funny and very flirty. Yes, he's abrupt, but in a jokey, flirty way.'

Rabbi Dunner is also unconvinced that there's any real cultural meaning to the Friday-night soirées for Charles Saatchi. 'I used to send Charles some of the happy-clappy audio tapes I make before the Holy Days so that people who come to the synagogue know the songs in advance, and a number of his friends rang and asked for copies. I think Charles's interest was ethnically motivated rather than anything else, but just as an interesting thing for him to play with for a while.' He thinks Nigella's interest is shallow too, and swiftly brought my attention to the number of pork recipes in her books.

'The Salmons were a great Jewish family – a bit like the Montefioris,' said Emily Lawson-Tancred when I asked her whether Nigella dropped into a bit of Yiddish every now and then. 'I never heard her talk about having anything to do with Jewishness until John came along. You only have to read *Feast* to see what she thinks about Jewishness nowadays. I think as you get older you get more interested in your roots, particularly when you're a parent.'

Sarah Johnson, a firm Catholic, agreed, and isn't at all surprised that Nigella includes Seder nights and Rosh

Hashana dinners in *Feast*. Nigella appears to be clutching her culture to her chest when she writes fondly, 'I can't think of any other faith that would lead one so directly to the deep-fat fryer, but then few religions express themselves so emphatically with food.' Sarah says, 'I think when you get past forty, you start to look a little deeper at things and feel more in need of your culture ... John was the first Jewish man she went out with. If you read her books, you'll see that she writes quite a lot about being Jewish, and that was something I'd never heard when she was younger.'

'The first time I'd been inside a synagogue was when John's grandmother died,' wrote Nigella in *Feast*, 'and I think that the fact that I married someone who's Jewish may be a sign that I wanted it to be more significant.' But Sarah added that Nigella is essentially a thinker rather than a follower, and will always exercise her own right to choose what she wants from her religion. 'I think that she and John flirted with the idea of going to synagogue, but her resistance to women sitting on a different level to the men put her off.' It's the culture rather than the religion that seems to have flicked her Jewish switch, and it was in *Feast*, a banquet of festival food for every culture, that she finally 'came out' as a true(ish) Jew. By this time – the book was published in 2004 – she had been married to not one but two Jews. The cast of characters that appears in all her books, popping in to advise on a recipe here, offer a golden tip there, is straight out of a Seder night: Granny Lawson, Great Aunts Myra and Frieda, sisters Horatia and Thomasina are all there, even Charles's late mother Daisy, and of course the great matriarch, Vanessa, her mother and mentor, all of them chopping and chatting, stirring and sighing as the feasts emerge, smelling of times gone by.

Perhaps it's because Sephardic cooking, the spiced lambs, rices and pulses of Saatchi's homeland, is so much more attractive than the dumplings and boiled chicken of the Ashkenazi old country, and so much more fun to cook, that she chose to explore the foods and festivals of her bloodline, or maybe it was, as Sarah Johnson said, a sign of maturity, of coming home to roost. Nigella would say that you are what you eat, and what better way to find the heart of a new love than through his own comfort food? Nigella writes in *Feast*, 'I can't pretend that I wasn't drawn towards this recipe from Daisy Iny's *Best of Baghdad Cooking* because of the fact that I am now married to a man who comes originally from the same place as the zalabia does. I think it's impossible to feel you know someone without a feeling for the food they ate as a child, or, at least, a curiosity about what they might have eaten.'

In *Nigella Bites* she tells us that she found the recipe for green coriander chutney in Claudia Roden's 'wonderful book of Jewish food'. She admits to spending wakeful nights at her computer, surfing on Amazon for new ways of spending her money on food books, and her bookshelves are chaotically packed with recipe books from all over the world. She was never going to be a ghetto Jew only interested in gefilte fish and bagels and worrying about whether or not her children would marry out – although by the time they're old enough it may be a different story.

Where most Brits would use breadcrumbs for salmon fish-cakes or chicken nuggets, she uses matzo meal, largely, she said, because she finds bought breadcrumbs 'horrible' and presumes that we all want the easy version. But matzo is an acquired taste, and there's a Jewish affection for it that its dry, tasteless quality doesn't quite merit. It was probably at her first mother-in-law's side that she discovered this little piece of Jewish symbolism. It's still used in the Seder night, the feast of Passover, to represent the bread that the Jews baked in the heat of the desert with flourless dough, hastily put together in their flight from Egypt. Anyone who grew up crawling under the Seder table in search of the hidden piece of matzo is going to have a different taste in their mouth when they plunge it into the haroset, a 'sludge of long-cooked dried fruit and nuts' that symbolizes the mortar the Jews used when building for their Egyptian masters.

Passover was Nigella's introduction to the feasts of the Jews, and it was around John's table that she learned to do 'the Jewish shrug' properly. John had just been diagnosed with cancer, and he wanted to celebrate this springtime festival as he had done as a child. Nigella said that it felt 'vaguely threatening, as if some alien force were making itself felt in my home'. She was now introduced to the dipping of the bitter herbs in salt water to celebrate the renewal of life among the tears of the Jews, the reading from the Haggadah (the gravy-stained Passover prayer book, passed down through the generations to retell the story each year) interspersed with prayers and the catchy ditty which follows all the tales of suffering with the refrain 'Day dahyenu' (roughly translated, 'Enough already').

Chicken soup is otherwise known as Jewish penicillin. It is what every Jewish mother gives her child, husband and neighbor when they so much as sneeze, and Nigella was returning to her roots when she included a recipe for it in *Nigella Bites*. 'That scientists have recently found chicken broth to contain anti-inflammatory and anti-bacterial properties is interesting for those on the lookout for non-patented fly remedies,' she writes, 'but true believers – culinary as much as devotional – never needed any such corroboration.' One of the oddest features of Friday nights, the weekly get-together of Jewish families, is that even in the most culinary of homes they will boil chicken. Boiling chicken gives off an unpleasant smell and produces a scum that could put you off chicken for years. But even Vanessa Salmon, dream of a cook, Jewless Jewess that she was, boiled her chicken.

Nigella said that she felt 'a bit squeamish' when she began following the rituals, and more than a little fraudulent. Jews of a certain age (over fifty) and class (middle- to upper-middle-class intellectuals in particular) often say they feel 'uncomfortable' when described as Jewish, or when grouped together and asked for their opinion on something that they could just as well respond to on an individual basis. Vanessa and Nigel certainly had little to do with their culture, and this may have left Nigella feeling uncomfortable about her heritage. But when she met John and his family her discomfort seems to have lifted somewhat. She is an intellectual, and there are probably still too many 'buts' for her to embrace the whole *megillah* (the whole works), but with Charles Saatchi leading the way to the Carlton Tower, it seems that Nigella is becoming less Jewish and more of a Jew.

For the majority of non-religious Jews across the world as

well as the increasing number of Jewish men 'marrying out' of the Jewish bloodline in the UK and America, there's a cultural dilemma. Those who want their children to experience the richness of their culture often feel fraudulent at the idea of teaching their children about Judaism when they don't believe in God, but for most Jews in the twenty-first century Judaism is not about God. Festivals can keep a culture alive, and this is certainly true of Judaism. 'After years of guilt about destroying the bloodline, I'm beginning to relax,' said a non-Jewish mother in a mixed marriage. 'I cook, they tell jokes and somehow there's a richness that comes from somewhere deep and unknowable. The kids understand instinctively.' Catholics, Hindus and Muslims will recognize the same dilemma, as well as the importance of a ritual family meal.

No wonder Nigella went straight to the top of the bestseller list when she taught us how to eat rather than cook; this Jewish mother was giving us so much more than food to nourish our souls. Interestingly, her literary agent, Ed Victor, has been trying to sell her and her books in Italy for years, but what does an Italian need with a cookbook? It's true that in Rome's larger bookshops there are a few shelves dedicated to cooking, but alongside the odd copy of *Un Uomo in Cucina* the only recipe books were filled with tips on Thai and Vietnamese cooking, chocolate and cocktails – evidence of globalization rather than anything else. When an Italian literary agent approached Ed Victor at the London Book Fair in 2005, it was with the intention of finally selling the Nigella phenomenon to Italy. However, Ed Victor's office refused to give any details of the deal.

However glorious the concept, Nigella may have been out of tune with mainstream British culture when she published *Feast* in 2003. Feasting is just not British, and Matthew Fort wondered when we would fit it all in. 'Sadly,' he wrote in the *Observer*, 'in this day and age, people do not seem to have the time or inclination to celebrate occasionally, let alone serially. But if we did, should we ever get round to doing so, this is the kind of food we can dream of cooking.' Others felt that Nigella was now out of sync with popular culture. Although *Feast* was chosen as one of twenty-four books likely to lure viewers away from Richard and Judy's book club on Channel Four to Jeremy Vine's on BBC's *Page Turners*, even the *Guardian* was bored with it. 'Her two-page introduction to Christmas manages forty "me"s and "I"s – as well as the phrase "Here is one that I made earlier", a reminder that one in ten of the recipes is recycled from her previous books,' complained Tom Jaine. '*Feast*'s coordinates are twelve calendar or life-cycle festivals (Jewish, Christian, Muslim, American), but there's much shoe-horning ("Kitchen Feasts", "Meatless Feasts", "Breakfast") to rake in other sorts of recipe, which rather destroys the point of it all. The single most annoying fact is that most of the recipes are for eight or ten people, which is spectacularly useless for most of her readers, who don't usually invite a dozen chums round for supper after the cinema on a Saturday and who really don't need the wince-worthy advice about serving caviar: "Just put the platters of food on the table and let people, stretchingly, help themselves. A bit of DIY is always relaxing at the table." A book for adepts; those of other faiths might throw up.'

When Roy Strong published a meaty volume in 2002, also

called *Feast*, subtitled *A History of Grand Eating*, the *Guardian* spat at her again. Ian Sansom delivered the poison: 'At a banquet held in Rome in 1513, apparently, the napkins were folded "so as to enclose a live bird which flew away when the napkin was opened by the guest",' he wrote, quoting Strong. 'Never mind Nigella: that really would be something to impress friends with this evening.'

Did she mind? Nigella had long ago made the distinction between her public and private selves, and quietly banked the checks. Besides, she had bigger fish to fry.

CHAPTER FIFTEEN

America

With the publication of *Feast* scheduled for the following year, it was time to try again to take the Nigella phenomenon to the hardest market of them all – America. It was a high-risk enterprise, and she had already failed when she tried to break into America two years earlier. Perhaps the time wasn't right, but it hadn't helped when she came out with statements like, 'The interesting thing about food is that it's both about reality and escape. After those planes bashed into the World Trade Center, I just wanted to chop something.'

It didn't help, either, that researchers at the University of Guelph in Ontario, Canada, were conducting a survey into the questionable hygiene of many TV chefs, and were scrutinizing food programs from Britain, the United States and Canada. They found that for every example of correct food handling there were thirteen food hygiene errors, or about seven per thirty-minute show. 'You cannot turn a home into a sterile environment,' Nigella retorted to the charge that her cooking was unhygienic. 'My childhood was spent eating food that had my mother's hair in it, and my children do the same. I have a hardy immune system. Perhaps that is thanks to the germs.'

At seventy-two years of age, the food writer Barbara Kafka has been around the food industry a long time. She is the author of twelve books on food, as well as *Vegetable Love* which comes out at Christmas 2005, and is a former US *Vogue* and *New York Times* columnist. She reminded me that Julia Child, a food icon to American viewers and readers since the 1950s, once dropped a chicken on the floor on TV, then served it up. 'Americans are not as puritanical as we're made out to be by the British press,' she said. She also warned me not to take the press accounts that Nigella had been dismissed by US critics as 'gastro-porn' too seriously, But it seemed that much of the US press was taking Nigella's flirtatious presentation at face value. 'Lawson's sexy round-ness mixed with her speed demon technique makes cooking dinner with Nigella look like a prelude to an orgy,' wrote the *New York Times* in 2001. Nigella's vampish alter ego, however, which had worked so well with British viewers, seemed to be too confronting for America. 'Food has to appeal. It has to, if you want, arouse appetite,' she purred to journal-ists. 'I mean, I don't mind if I'm accused of a, you know, culinary come-on.' Was straitlaced America ever going to be as entranced by Nigella's sexy, instinctive cooking? Her American publisher even tried to pin her down on measure-ments: 'I had put on a recipe, "sprinkle with parsley",' she remembered. ' "How much?" my American publisher asked. I say, "What business is it of mine how much parsley?" '

Marlena Spieler is a food writer and columnist for the *San Francisco Chronicle*. She said that although a huge splash in

Gourmet magazine proclaiming her as an It Girl, and a show on America's *House and Garden* TV station raised her profile, Nigella just didn't happen in 2001. Maybe it was just that her heart wasn't in it after John's death. Or did she need success too much, still unsure of her future with her new love, Charles Saatchi? Whatever it was, the American public didn't want to know. Nigella gave up and went home. She'd already made £4 million from her TV and writing empire by that time, and she was finding the company of her new boyfriend increasingly comforting.

But by 2003, it was time to try again. Jamie Oliver had cracked America with his Britpot laddish cooking, and it seemed that this time Nigella's impeccable British manners and sexy older woman image might be just what Americans were looking for. Could America offer the success that was beginning to fade in Britain?

When she went back to the USA it was with the confidence of a woman who didn't need America quite as much as she once had. Barbara Kafka said, 'She had honed her own sense of self by that time.' She took with her a new wardrobe of décolleté evening gowns, and somehow there were far fewer lines on her face than she had had around the time of John's death. Flirting with high-profile presenters on the chatterati circuit, she set off on a whistle-stop tour of the major shows. What had been dismissed the first time round as 'gastro-porn' was suddenly embraced – quite literally, as Jay Leno graduated from innuendo to clinch. When she asked him to help her tie up the joint of pork she had smeared with onion and herbs, he lowered his gaze and purred suggestively, 'Are we still talking about the meat?'

He put his arms around her waist and began to carve the joint, bringing out a kittenish quality in Nigella which had not been seen since the earliest days of *Nigella Bites*.

'She's sexy, and sexy is always good,' said Barbara Kafka, who is also a former presenter on the Food Channel. 'Especially on TV. It's an interesting persona for someone to take. When you go on TV, you choose your garments, and she chooses low-cut, tight-fitting sweaters which for someone who's not exactly a waif makes a certain kind of statement. She is genuinely sexy, but in real life probably no more so than you or I.'

According to Marlena Spieler, what it takes to be successful in America is an English accent, good looks and a big-budget PR campaign. She also reckons that Saatchi & Saatchi may have played a part in Nigella's success. 'I remember reading all the papers in 2003 and you could just see that it all came from a very good set of press releases,' she said. 'There was a definite PR twist to it. The whole tour was very slick, very well coordinated and had PR written all over it.'

She was even invited to cook for President Bush when he visited Tony Blair at Downing Street in November 2003. The menu included a starter of roast pumpkin, radicchio and feta salad, followed by braised Norfolk ham with a honey and mustard glaze, creamed baked potatoes and seasonal vegetables, followed by double apple pie with a Cheddar crust accompanied by vanilla ice cream or custard. The President was charmed.

Nigella had spent her life surrounded by opportunities, handed to her on a plate by her friends and colleagues. From

Oxford through to the UK's most influential newspapers to the Groucho Club and John's influential media network, she had always made good use of her contacts. She didn't abuse her high-powered friends, but they gave her a natural step up. She is, as her friend Sarah Johnson says, a 'noble woman'. She was now married to the most influential advertising guru the world had ever seen, with a vast fortune, considerable contacts and time to play with. Why *wouldn't* Nigella allow him to give her access to the most lucrative of all markets?

Her campaign brought her an enormously high profile. The *San Francisco Chronicle*, winner of the 2004 James Beard Award for the Best Newspaper Food Section, ran a cover story on her, and its influential editor Phil Bronstein invited Nigella to his home for dinner. Bronstein was married at the time to Sharon Stone, and according to Spieler (who worked for him) he even showed Nigella around Sharon's closet. 'I don't know if she tried the shoes on, but I would have done if I were her.'

As Barbara Kafka pointed out, even a food icon like Julia Child, who had for years been inspiring home cooks with books like *Mastering the Art of French Cooking*, didn't really shift a lot of copies until she was on TV. 'She was one of the original voices on US TV, along with Graham Kerr, Constance Spry's partner, Elsie Cook and Dione Lucas. She was the food goddess of the 1950s. Everyone knew who she was. People would line up around the block for her signings. She would have been the equivalent of the captain of the girls' hockey team, someone who all the girls would have adored. She had a special kind of quality about her. She was very intelligent, and was very well connected.' Although

Nigella was no Julia, according to Kafka, neither of them would ever have made it in America without a TV deal, and when *Nigella Bites* was snapped up by the small fashion, beauty and home entertaining cable channels Style and E, she instantly became a star. Not that Marlena Spieler thinks it was such a big deal. 'You could put a talking donkey on TV here and if it had an English accent it would become a star. *Two Fat Ladies* could not have been more popular. I remember Jamie Oliver doing a Thanksgiving recipe, and he was stuffing the neck cavity, something that we wouldn't ordinarily do here, but what he was doing with the food was totally irrelevant because of his accent.'

'The accent is good,' said Kafka, 'but you've got to have the content too. Jamie stuffs the neck of the turkey – that's different, it's surprising. Nigella doesn't do that. What she does is rather boring. We've seen it all before.'

'Britishness' was popular in North America at this time, though no one was quite sure why. 'It could be the influence of BBC America, which gained big audiences during the Iraq war; or of British magazine editors such as Anna Wintour and Tina Brown; or of Madonna's transformation into a welly-wearing, gun-totin', rambler-baiting member of the country set,' wrote Jemima Lewis in the *Telegraph*. 'Whatever the explanation, we are almost embarrassingly fashionable. Nike is about to bring out a range of trainers in Harris tweed. British restaurants and gastro-pubs are springing up all over New York. Nigella Lawson and Jamie Oliver are daring to teach the Americans how to cook. Most startling of all, Americans are copying our speech patterns.'

Everyone seemed to want a bite of Nigella. She was offered

a regular food column for the *New York Times*, and *Gourmet* and *Bon Appetit* were also knocking at her agent's door. The *New York Times* was the big prize. 'It was her defining moment. It's *the* national newspaper,' explained Marlena. 'It's sold across the country and has great snob value. It's quite lefty, and for anyone who doesn't want to be thought of as parochial it's a must.' 'It was a good gig,' admitted Barbara Kafka, who wrote for the same pages until 1999.

Vanity Fair columnist Michael Wolff said she had become a household name in the homes that counted: 'Her regular Wednesday column in the *New York Times* certainly helps to propel her into her position of influence. She's very well plugged in. She certainly knows a lot of the people I know.' Barbara Kafka agreed. 'You have to remember that she has a husband who's a very well connected media figure, and you have to admire the way she has handled herself.' She warned against looking too far ahead, though. As a columnist who, she says, 'sloped off into the night' from the *New York Times*, she has seen what happens when a new editor takes over the hot seat. 'New editors want to bring their people in with them. They want younger people, new stars. I've seen people come and go many times. If she lost that column, she's well connected enough, she would probably find something else to do.'

With *Nigella Bites* on Style and E and her column syndi cated across 600 provincial papers in the US, Nigella seeme to be everywhere. And this time the critics loved her. 'Nigell brings you into her life and tells you how she thinks abou food, how meals come together in her head ... and how sh cooks for family and friends ... A breakthrough ... wit hundreds of appealing and accessible recipes,' wrote Amanc

Hesser in the *New York Times*. 'Nigella Lawson serves up irony and sensuality with her comforting recipes ... she's the Queen of Come-On Cooking,' cheered the *Los Angeles Times*. 'A chatty, sometimes cheeky, celebration of home-cooked meals,' wrote *USA Today*. All this was a far cry from the *Dallas Morning News*'s initial pronouncement: 'Nigella's attractiveness far outweighs her cooking skills.'

She was the English rose with the cut glass accent who cooked like a dream, and could always be counted on for a bit of tongue-in-cheek naughtiness, something that all TV producers lust after. 'Nigella is seen as a cute English girl, and she is always being invited on to food shows,' Marlena Spieler said. 'I remember that there was one show where they took twenty chefs away for a weekend in Aspen, and she wore a T-shirt with "English Muffin" written on it. I thought that was cute. She knows how to play the game, oh God does she!'

Nigella files her column for the *New York Times* from Eaton Square every fortnight, and pops over just often enough to ensure her future in the States for the time being. Susan Spungen, a food writer and food editor for *Martha Stewart Living*, believes that anyone who writes a seminal work like *How to Eat* has a place in America, even if the rest of her books were perceived as 'shallow'. She and Spieler both noticed that all the attention was on *How to Eat*. 'All the big newspapers covered her at that time,' said Spieler, 'but I noticed that not so many covered *Feast* when that came out here. Certainly the *San Francisco Chronicle* didn't cover it.'

Barbara Kafka disputed the idea that *How to Eat* was ever seen as a seminal work. 'The focus on the family, the richness of the memories – that's par for the course in America. *The*

River Café Cook Book had more of an impact here. There was nothing innovative in *How to Eat* as far as Americans were concerned. I think she's intelligent in using recipes that most people can do, that are familiar. They're possibly a little too familiar. She doesn't offer much surprise, but they work well.'

Kafka compared Heston Blumenthal with the Roux Brothers to illustrate what 'seminal' means to her: 'The Roux Brothers contributed nothing new but were very important and made a lot of money. Heston was a British-born physicist – he was properly innovative and he got his Michelin stars in a way that was quite unlike the way the Roux got theirs.' She thinks that the mark of a truly seminal work is how long it stays in print. 'Mrs. Beeton wrote books that provide information that you can trust, that people can make sense of. Tante Marie is still selling in France. Constance Spry is still around. So are Jane Grigson and Elizabeth David.'

She warned that food culture is changing across the Western world. 'In America the chef is now the food writer. Perhaps they're assisted by someone. Things are very transitory. Madhur Jaffrey, Ken Hom – they were really big names in the UK. Jill Dupleix and Terry Durack were everywhere in Australia, and then they moved to the UK and you never really hear about Jill any more. It's a shame.'

Chris Styler is a New York chef who also writes for *Family Circle*, *New York Magazine* and *Good Food*, and is Editor-at-Large for *Food Arts* magazine. He agreed that chefs are becoming literary and TV stars, but that there's a big difference in what they are trying to convey. 'It seems to me that what's happening in the world of well-known chefs is that there are those chefs/cooks who provide entertainment and those that provide authentic cooking and a link with something bigger than the food itself – family, friends, sharing and giving. The two camps, of course, are not mutually exclusive.' He thinks Nigella's cooking is about the latter. 'I think the reason behind Nigella's success is her ability to convey the importance of food and cooking in her own life, without making it seem like a life or death issue. It's refreshing to watch someone who is less concerned with getting it absolutely right than with putting good food on the table.'

The *New York Times* column alone would never have been enough to ensure Nigella's success, according to Spungen. She needed the TV profile, and now that *Nigella Bites* and *Forever Summer* have fallen off the schedules she's going to need a new show to keep her in the public consciousness. 'Her column in the *New York Times* lacks the pizazz of her TV programs and *How to Eat*,' Spungen said. 'In the beginning it was run with her picture next to it, but they dropped it, and it seems like she's not really there any more. Her recipes don't always thrill. She is one of the major players because of it, but people will always prefer to see her on TV. Americans love an English accent, and she's wonderfully haughty. It's like she's above the rest of us, and we like that. We don't want to relate to her, although her personal tragedies humanize her. People here know that she lost her husband to cancer.'

America already has its own domestic goddess in former model Martha Stewart, and even her entanglement in a fraud scandal failed to spoil America's appetite for her. Nigella's strength lay in being absolutely nothing like Stewart. 'I am so the opposite of what she's about, because

I'm not about the quest to perfect your life and to make everything in it beautiful and shiny. You know, I'm a bit more, "Oh come on. We'll just do it this way, you know? Let's do it in half an hour," ' she told the endless queue of chat-show hosts who made the inevitable comparison.

Barbara Kafka, who likes Nigella enormously, said that there's a fundamental difference between her and Martha. 'Martha's a really nasty piece of work, although I do admire her as a businesswoman. Strictly speaking Martha knows very little about food. She stole a lot of her recipes. In cookery terms, plagiarism can only be about the language. She's so lazy. In cookery terms you can only be accused of plagiarism when you steal the language, and yet she didn't even bother to change the words when she stole from a friend of mine – I mean sixty pages. She had to pay up when she was found out. She doesn't even see why she shouldn't be able to get away with it.'

Spungen suggested that to compare Nigella with Stewart was to miss the point. 'Nigella is sexy and alluring but I'm not sure that people take her seriously. She's a celebrity rather than a food pundit. When she's invited to appear on *Today* about the South Beach Festival or something, I think it's because people like to see her. They know she writes about food, but they like to look at her. I guess I think of her as being niche here, maybe not being completely garish. I was surprised to see the glamour shots of her in white fur on her website – that's not going to help if she wants to be seen as a serious food writer.' She thinks that it's her genuine interest in food that she should play on. 'I was sitting next to her at the Wolsey [in London's Piccadilly] and she was snuggled in next to Charles Saatchi. She's really beautiful up close, and I loved the way that she was tucking into her mashed potatoes. I thought, yup, she's the real thing.'

'It's very hard to be so successful here,' Michael Wolff explained, 'to go from a discrete line to having a big business. Martha did a big deal with a retailer, and went public. You need a lot of investment to be that big.' He reckons that Nigella is second only to Martha in 'home-making' in the States. 'She's built herself a very serious career here,' he said. 'The spheres of these kinds of career are thrown into imbalance because of Martha – everything in cookery and home-making is overshadowed by her. But take Martha out of the equation and Nigella would be leading the high end of the home-making market.' And that's without really working at it. She doesn't seem to be working at it as hard as she might. 'I know Martha and she is a real businesswoman. I just don't get the feeling that Nigella is that dedicated, or that Charles would really want her to be.'

Nigella's Living Kitchen range is available now across the USA, offering designer mixing bowls in duck-egg blue or soul white, an 'organic droplet shaped' colander in shiny stainless steel and Nigella's personal favorite, a 'handbag'-sized whisk. An ingenious wood chopping board with hidden aluminium tray and a ceramic bread bin with cutting-board top are some of the more useful items, and for the domestic goddess who has everything (including the time to bake) there's even the duck-egg-blue shopping list pad with matching pencil. 'Only those who get through life by writing lists will know how crucial these pads and pencils are,' writes Nigella on her website, seemingly without a hint of irony. 'The paper is long enough, like an old-fashioned shopping list pad, to get everything down, and because the back is sticky you can put it on the fridge, on your wallet or hang it from your computer to add to as you work.'

'The pieces look as good as they work,' cooed Deanna Larson in *Nashville City*, one of hundreds of provincial city papers across America to lap up whatever Nigella was offering. 'Designed by Lawson and Sebastian Conran, they look like things grabbed out of a drawer or shelf to measure something in a pinch, which is a lot like how Nigella cooks on TV.' 'They're nothing new,' said Kafka. 'When Elizabeth David brought French cooking equipment to Britain, that was new. That made a real difference to the way that people cooked. The handbag-sized whisk, the chopping board with drawer – they already exist on the market.'

Marlene Spieler did spot some tear-shaped glass which look remarkably similar to Nigella's in an American glassware series from the 1930s.

'I'm not altogether comfortable with the notion of becoming a brand,' Nigella said of the Living Kitchen range. 'I feel absolutely fine about having my name associated with cooking and the home when it's with my readers and viewers, because they get the point of me – someone who simply enjoys food and cooking and who is interested in the role food plays in our lives. But I get uncomfortable when I'm on some show and the announcer says, "We have with us the domestic goddess." I just want to cringe because that's not what I am. I guess it's my own fault. I find it very odd how the world craves an expert so much that they want to turn you into one even when you're not. Somehow, in this hallowed world of TV, everything goes right. But in reality, that's not true.'

Nigella may not even pretend to be interested in taking over Martha Stewart's role, but food pundits and viewers can't help but speculate. And there are plenty of other contenders waiting in the wings. 'I think Rachel Ray is more likely to be the main contender,' suggested Marlena. 'She's cute, bubbly and young enough. She's got a show on the Food Network and her own magazine too. Nigella is a big shot, but she's one of many.' Ray was born into a family of restaurateurs and grew up in the kitchen. 'My first vivid memory is watching Mom in a restaurant kitchen,' she said. 'She was flipping something with a spatula. I tried to copy her and ended up grilling my right thumb. I was three or four,' said Ray. 'Everyone on both sides of my family cooks.'

New York foodie Caitlin Goldschmidt took to the streets of Manhattan to gather opinions on Nigella's success from her target market, the food-loving mom. She felt it was Nigella's column in the *New York Times* that gave her the most cachet. 'Although the *Times* is the New York paper, upscale people around the country subscribe to it, so appearing in it immediately made her name known to a large number of people. I don't know how she wangled the *New York Times* gig. It makes her credible as a foodie, although serious New York foodies look down their noses at her a bit. Her recipes convey old-fashioned home-made quality, comfort food, which appeals to Americans who tend to be suspicious of upscale, fussy food. Her recipes seem forgiving – they come off as a bit imprecise – you don't have to worry if you don't get it exact, and she comes off as reassuring. She's also offering sexy fun food in an era of no-carb restrictions and she definitely has style, but it's relaxed and warm.'

Caitlin thinks Nigella has charisma and a uniquely recognizable vibe. 'She's gorgeous and sexy but women can still relate to her – she doesn't seem perfect. Maybe she's what we dream of being – a sexy food goddess, curvy with a little extra flesh, seducing our men in the kitchen with mouth-watering home cooking. Her British thing also makes her distinctive and memorable. On the other hand, her personal history could possibly be a turn-off for some Americans, and make her sexiness seem more threatening.' However, Caitlin thought that most Americans were probably unaware of her background.

'She's the anti Martha Stewart. When you think of Martha, you think of an immaculate and exquisitely tasteful kitchen (be it Turkey Hill or Alexis Stewart's loft) with tiny perfect hors d'oeuvres laid out on a plate. When you think of Nigella, you imagine a warm but maybe slightly messy kitchen, stove covered with pots, wine flowing among a gathering of friends. Maybe one of the pots is boiling over, but who cares? She looks like the kind of woman who would stick her finger in the food for a taste (whereas Martha would use a spoon). On the other hand, Martha Stewart comes off a bit like an upscale Emily Post type who will guide you gently toward elegance, perhaps a bit frosty, but her lack of in-your-face sexuality is calming in a way.'

Caitlin's friend Robin Sellier had not watched her TV programs or even bought her book, but she was one of the few she talked to who had a very positive impression of Nigella. She loved the aspiration she offers. 'She makes it seem like a higher quality of life is accessible. It's a mix of old-fashioned made-from-scratch quality but done in a stylish way and done easily and accessibly.' She regularly uses the recipes in Nigella's column and finds them excellent, especially the spring lamb and the chocolate pinwheels.

Caitlin's seventy-two-year-old mother, Julie Jones, loves to eat at Nobu and Bobby Flay. She reads Nigella's column, but has found her recipes disappointing. 'She sells well because the pictures are good, as well as the layout of the cookbook and the recipes sound like they would be simple and easy to make. The recipes seem to center on comfort food like "my grandmother's bread pudding", but when you make the recipes they don't really deliver.' 'She has a unique look,' said Nancy Cincotta, a former caterer. 'She's sexy and she made food sexy in a no-carb era, which gave people permission to eat and enjoy themselves. No one else is currently coming across that way, plus she's marketed well.' Nancy doesn't really see Nigella as a 'food type': 'She's not really bringing anything new to the table, but she has a homey and simple vibe that people like.'

Jane Hassler lives in the suburbs and watches a lot of cookery shows on TV, particularly the Italian-oriented Lidia Bastianich and Michael Chiarello. 'I can't stand Nigella,' she said. 'I don't like her choice of ingredients. They're fattening and they often have a short shelf life that I'll never use again in any other recipe. I think it's a kind of heavier, grander food she's pushing.' She found her TV persona 'standoffish, not warm and fuzzy. Neither is Martha Stewart, but at least she doesn't come across as holier than thou and her basic recipes are more practical to actually make.'

As a professional cook, Chris Styler said, 'I enjoy Nigella's style for her unique voice and her ability to write vividly about food. If I were a less experienced cook I imagine I would be convinced by her show and her books that I could do what she does – and that is no mean feat in a nation of non-cooks intimidated by the thought of facing a range or an oven.'

Happy to have found a place at the American dinner table, Nigella turned down offers in 2004 to do more TV and personal appearances in America, and rumors inevitably began to fly again that this had to do with starting a family with Saatchi. 'One of the reasons I turned something like this down earlier this year,' said the ever pragmatic Nigella, 'is because I have two lovely young children, and I don't like to travel all the time.' Selling books can be an arduous business of signings and media interviews, and she was keen to keep control wherever possible. In the UK it had been easier. 'I don't stay overnight when I'm touring,' she said. 'I might be out for a day but my kids know I'm around. I do plea bargaining with them,' she jokes. 'I tell them it's not for ever and that other mommies go out and come back very late too. It's not the ideal way to do it, but it's a compromise. When I go abroad I have to start saying sorry earlier.'

CHAPTER SIXTEEN

Cop shows and Chinese slippers

Nigella's life is filled with new friends, leaving some old friends 'terribly sad' at being dropped. Olivia Lichtenstein wrote about the kind of girly days and nights they used to have Before Charles in her article in *Eve*. 'We quite happily sit up until 4 a.m., drinking and chatting and revelling in our middle youth, while we push to one side all thoughts of the terrible hangovers that await us.' 'We never run out of things to say,' agreed Nigella. 'Women don't mind having the same conversation again and again. We're gripped with equal fascination each time.' Olivia has not moved up into the new circle of friends, and after spending two years charting John's illness for her BBC documentary, sharing hangovers and children's sleepovers, she declined to be interviewed for this book about it.

The celebrity stage is one on which mere mortals are simply not invited to tread, and even if the celebrities themselves have kept their feet on the ground, their old friends seem to distance themselves, adopting a reverence not normally afforded to their peers. Sarah Johnson, who had been a good friend since Oxford, who shared wedding days with Nigella and John, whose eldest boy John snuggled up with to read *The Cat in the Hat* before he had a little boy of his own, was 'touched' when Nigella made a point of saying hello at the theatre recently. 'I'd got some really good seats for *The Producers* to thank my brother-in-law, who is the chairman of Channel Four, for some favors that he'd done for me, and I'd taken my son and his friend with us. I got a tap on the shoulder and it was Nigella leaning two rows across to say hello. She was way the most famous person there, but that's the kind of person she is. Charles Saatchi was sitting next to her with his nose in the program. He's probably shy but it seems that he's very rude.'

She doesn't bear a grudge. 'She's a sweet person who I don't see as much as I used to since she got rich. There are whole areas of our lives that don't cross over any more, and maybe when you live with a multi-millionaire you just don't really see your old friends as much. I'm not sure that I could keep up enough to keep the friendship going. I think if she wanted to know anything about getting her children into a Catholic school she might ring me for advice, but that's hardly likely, is it?'

Emily Lawson-Tancred is among the few still having lunch with her 'fairly regularly', thirty years on from the Godolphin and Latymer days, but she has never met Saatchi. 'I've always preferred to see my friends on a one-to-one anyway,' she said loyally. She sees her friend as unchanged, apart from the attempt at discretion forced upon people in the public eye who can't go out for lunch without being recognized.

Life has settled into a domestic if reclusive pattern set by Saatchi. Nigella seems to follow her men into their world, from the dangerous sports weekends of Hubie Gibb to the upwardly-mobile networking John favored and now to the quiet elegance of the Saatchi life, padding around in their Chinese slippers, tucking into bagels in bed over a TV cop show or *University Challenge*. 'He loves it when I do cook but he's really not very interested,' she said of Saatchi in a peculiar echo of John. 'I think he would very often rather have a bowl of cereal.'

Saatchi's biographer and Nigella's former boss, Ivan Fallon, can't imagine two people being more different. 'Charles doesn't like books – he never reads, and doesn't particularly like food,' he said, 'but they do seem to love each other.' The woman whom Fallon once thought was deeply introverted when she first came to work for him at the *Sunday Times* has joined Saatchi in his reclusiveness. 'I think it's important to feel that your life takes place in private at home,' Nigella has said. 'I've got a date in my agenda in two months' time, and I'm thinking, "Oh my God, I have to go out on Saturday in eight weeks." '

After the years in which her every move was served up for public consumption, and John was chronicling every gruesome moment of his illness in his columns, after the BBC *Inside Story* documentary and the play *A Lump in My Throat*, Nigella, the once 'almost autistic child', seems to have found her level. 'I would hate to say that I'm having the time of my life,' she told Jane Gordon in the *Mail on Sunday*, 'because I would hate to diminish any other part of it, but I finally feel like myself. I don't struggle so much; even the fact that I go up and down as a person doesn't frighten me. Sometimes, like all women, I will feel, for no reason, that I don't look good, and I find myself saying to Charles, "Oh, I hate these fleshy bits on my thighs." And he will say to me, "But those are the bits I like the best." And it's strange, but now I am less self-conscious than at any other time in my life. And that is the great gift from Charles.'

She is 'gloriously in love' with Charles. 'Nothing makes you more alive than being in love,' she said. 'Charles is divine, incredibly cosy, not at all like his image,' she told the *Daily Mail*'s Lynda Lee-Potter. 'He's kind, funny, good-looking, and so solid to hold. I love the feel of him.' She describes him as 'enormously alive with passionate energy. I love that.' She also loves his devotion to his daughter, Phoebe, and the way he leaves his cell phone on at all times in case she needs him. For a child who doesn't get a mention in her own father's memoirs, that's impressive stuff. 'We're existing in a disgusting, loved-up environment,' she told Lydia Slater in the *Evening Standard*. 'I did a lot of parties, which is why I don't need to now.' They spend their summers in Tuscany where, she wrote in her column in the *New York Times*, they love 'the simplicity'. The simple villa they rent is a bargain at £15,000 a week.

Her selection of records on BBC's *Desert Island Discs* gives a fascinating insight into what their world sounds like, a blend of Chemical Brothers (the remix) and 'Daddy Cool' by Boney M. She loves the transcendental power of music. 'The primitive thing about music is to put you into an ecstatic state,' she said, and it's Charles who keeps her informed. 'I really love being with an older man who keeps me up to date with contemporary music,' she told Sue Lawley. She prefers upbeat music. 'I don't want to be thinking, "Oh, aren't these lyrics sad?" I want to be taken out of myself and made to feel fantastic,' she told *Word* magazine. 'I loved those early Mary J Blige songs that just make you want to dance. Music should to be bigger than you. I love disco, I like "Hey Boy Hey Girl" by the Chemical Brothers, Eminem, the remix of "Blue Monday" by New Order that came out a few years ago, "Yeke Yeke" by Mory Kante ... those kind of things. There are things I like from my youth too, like "Come Up and See Me". One of my fantasies is to do a version of that, in my next career as a singing superstar. I want Dr Dre to produce me.'

Andrew Harrison of *Word* magazine asked her about the rumor that she had been spotted clubbing in Ibiza just after John died. 'I did,' she confessed. 'We went to Pacha, but only because my friend said, "We can't do this, we're forty," and I then wanted to prove to her that it's all in your head. "Look, I'll show you." But things were all rather hellish in my life then. We were all, in a rather frenzied way, trying to have a fabulous time to take our minds off it. That's not really the person I am – I'm actually quite shy. So it was all rather dancing on the deck while the ship is sinking.'

As John did with her, Nigella too seems to have brought out the best in Charles. She accepts that he is the complete opposite to John, famously shy, refusing to go to his own parties – he relied on her to host the opening of his latest gallery in County Hall on his behalf. She did it happily, in the role John had played for her, this time clad in Vivienne Westwood and draped around exotic celebrities such as Salman Rushdie and his partner, Padma Lakshmi. 'He doesn't like parties,' she explained at the time. 'He hates socializing and he'd have had a horrible time. It would have been much harder to do with him hanging around saying, "Can we go home now?" '

Charles's first wife Doris explained his shy persona as the diffident introversion that comes with a certain kind of immigrant. 'I'd say that his extreme regard for privacy and withdrawal from the public eye has something to do with the fact that his family were immigrants escaping persecution in Iraq,' she said. Compare that with the showy extroversion of the second-generation immigrant in John Diamond, and the solid sense of self of the totally established Nigella. Time and success have given him the confidence to stop trying to assimilate into his adopted culture, as Doris said, by marrying blondes like Kay and herself. 'I think what we felt for one another was the pull of the dark towards the light and the longing of the light for darkness.' Nigella's place as a dark Jewish socialite deeply plugged into the infrastructure of British society is the final dream of every aspirant Jew. If that doesn't make him relax enough to be seen at his own parties, surely nothing will.

She is finally happy. I see her twirling wildly with her kids to Wheatus's 'Teenage Dirtbag' in her signature long black skirt and trainers, singing along to 'Sugar Sugar' – badly despite the attempts of her singing teacher – and fantasizing about her debut single, something from *Tosca*, produced by Dr Dre. And perhaps, when everyone is in bed asleep, she dances to Mori Kante's 'Yeke Yeke' as she once did with John.

CHAPTER SEVENTEEN

The next course

By 2005 the celebrity-chef culture has changed much of the eating habits in the UK in little more than ten years. In 1998 Delia Smith's *How to Cook* series on the BBC resulted in an extra 1.3 million eggs being sold in Britain each day. By the turn of the century Nigella and Jamie both had TV shows that peaked at 5 million, this in a nation of 55 million where the top soaps attract 21 million. The doors of perception seemed to be opening and showing us a world of new possibilities with food. Supermarket profits showed that even the least confident were choosing gourmet ready meals, while a steady stream of able cooks were taking their oven gloves to the next level.

One in four adults said they were much more confident about their cooking than they used to be. 'Thanks to the pan-rattling of Jamie Oliver, Nigella Lawson, Delia Smith, Gordon Ramsay and a host of other TV chefs, Britains are turning away from meat-and-two-veg. or ready meals and becoming culinary adventurers,' wrote Patrick Barkham and Audrey Gillan in the *Guardian*. 'Almost six in ten consumers feel their cooking habits have been influenced by the legion of celebrity chefs, while only 20 per cent say they have not changed what meals they cook in the last five years. More than a quarter of adults say they have tried a new recipe, and one in five claims that watching cookery programs on TV has encouraged them to try different food. Almost three in ten (31 per cent) say they used a wider variety of ingredients than they used to, and just under one in four (24 per cent) say they buy and use better-quality ingredients than they used to.'

By 2005 we had turned into a nation of dinner-party hosts. 'Gurus from Nigella Lawson to Jamie Oliver have enticed the country's households to spend a remarkable £39.5 billion a year on dishing out the likes of Thai prawns and sugar snaps at home rather than paying to eat them at restaurants,' wrote Martin Wainwright in the *Guardian*. 'A poll of 1,007 adults by the Prudential group found that the average British household now hosts 14 full-scale dinner parties a year, even if some take place relatively informally in front of a TV program.'

However, Nigella's aspirational message was sometimes more powerful than her have-a-go philosophy. 'Although the teachings of Delia, Nigella and co. are put into action by many domestic cooks, 12 per cent of dinner party hosts cheat by passing off pre-prepared or caterers' food as their own work. The survey estimates that the average annual household bill for giving dinner parties is £1,036, much cheaper than comparable prices for eating out.' And would-be cooks aged twenty-five to thirty-five were the most likely group to be influenced by celebrity chefs, the report claimed.

The re-runs of *Nigella Bites* on the cable channels were

already beginning to look old-fashioned in our reality-obsessed TV culture, despite the glimpses they gave us of Nigella's world. Food programs have followed *Big Brother* into a formula based on game shows and bad language, forcing TV producers to take them out of the kitchen, even out of a lifestyle, and dangle their fortunes in front of an audience interested only in winning or losing. Chefs, unknown or otherwise, show us what it takes to launch their dream kitchens in a frighteningly short period of time and with precarious bank balances. *Kitchen Nightmares* allows Gordon Ramsay to use the kind of language reserved for teenage trainee chefs as he whips restaurateurs and chefs out of their complacency and tinned foodstuffs into using Michelin-style techniques and local produce. *Hell's Kitchen* uses the same formula: celebrities and punters, who look as though they have never been in the kitchen, pitch themselves against each other in a gastro cook-off under the tutelage of our best-looking chefs. Rather than focusing on ingredients and techniques we should have learned about as children, TV presumes that we now know the rules and have leap-frogged directly to chef level.

The Times Magazine's food detective, Sheila Keating, summed up our astonishment when Gary Rhodes threw a superstar tantrum in the 2005 series and closed his reality TV restaurant, 'leaving celebrity diners (mostly from other TV shows) faint with hunger. "None of us was good enough to be putting out Michelin-starred food," he pronounced. It wasn't so much the stating of the obvious that got me but how confused we seem to be about food, restaurants and celebrity these days; how much spin and style wins out over substance … If the characters [Rhodes] was in charge of had really been able to turn out food to Michelin standards after a few days, it would have made a mockery of the youngsters inconspicuously and industriously learning from the masters of real kitchens such as Georgio Locatelli, Richard Corrigan or Michel Roux Jnr, talented trainees who could never imagine being given a prize worth £250,000 to start their own restaurant.'

Just as we were losing our fear about getting back into the kitchen, shows like *Hell's Kitchen* were implying that it's all about looking good, and defied us to offer guests a simple risotto primavera again. However, the British have always been fashion leaders, and we deal with food – now that we've discovered it again – in the same way that we treat a hem length or a shade of green. Can we really use capers for a dinner party for twelve these days? Aren't they too Delia? Shouldn't we be more Moro now? Nigella saw it coming in *How to Eat*. 'Just because a food is no longer flavor of the month,' she scolded, 'it shouldn't follow that it is evermore to be spoken of as a shameful aberration.' Her voice was drowned out by the endless waves of food fads, and the nation's long-held habit of taking a ride on them.

Nigella has done much more than she had set out to do. From a freelance job in a niche magazine to writing what many critics see as a seminal work, Nigella Lawson became one of the most influential people in British cookery of the twenty-first century. She defined cookery in a way that no one had been able to do before. 'Nigella has made cooking the new sex,' wrote Hadley Freeman in the *Guardian*. She wrote *How to Eat* to breathe life again into her mother and sister, and let their powerful influence on her spread out into the world. She couldn't have known that there were so many people ready to listen to her mother's wise words, and to re-create the kitchens of their own childhoods in a heady mix of nostalgia and need. But perhaps John did realize this.

Her confidence has increased over the years, and her books are brimming over with stories and people from her past, not only recalling her own youth, but adding a richness to the recipes and a dimension to her writing her mother would surely have approved of, and an upbeat quality that would make Thomasina smile.

She has used her work to help her through a series of terrible tragedies, and she has emerged balanced, emotion-ally articulate and fulfilled. She has learned that helping herself is healthy and that, rather than being a cardinal sin, greed can be good. Her British stoicism and Jewish sensu-ality, her nobility of spirit and kindness of heart have endeared her to a wider audience than she could ever have imagined.

Of course, her legacy is at the fickle mercy of our popular culture. In an increasingly celebrity-obsessed Britain, Nigella is probably no more than a TV phenomenon, the gastro-porn queen riding a one-trick pony. She filled a gap with her sexy allure and her finger-licking cooking, but it could never last. If America's skill is to recognize opportunity for what it is, her success over there showed her for exactly what she was – a posh, sexy woman with a twinkle in her eye and a hostess trolley full of stories to tell.

Her beauty has had an undeniable influence on her success, and as this book was going to press *Harpers and*

Queen announced that the forty-five-year-old Nigella was still in the top ten of the world's most beautiful women. Angelina Jolie topped the list followed by Christy Turlington, Queen Raina of Jordan, Sofia Coppola, Nigella Lawson, Uma Thurman, Emmanuelle Beart, Kate Moss, Aishwarya Rai and Princess Charlotte of Monaco at number 10.

So what does the future hold for Nigella Lawson? She's had her kitchenware range on the market since 2002, the collection of Sebastian Conran-designed spoons, whisks and pestle and mortars for the person who has everything. 'I can't live without a small whisk which can fit in my handbag,' said Nigella, with the air of a woman who lives with art installations in the spare room. At the time of writing, her ITV daytime chat show *Nigella* was due to be broadcast every day throughout July 2005, and was being billed as a stylish, glossy, intelligent chat over lunch with her super-celebrity guest of the day. Apparently the behind-the-scenes VIP treatment for guests is not just an unusually large fee, but goodie bags packed with expensive products, individually picked by Nigella, not to mention hand massages in the Green Room.

'We're trying to avoid anything too formulaic but there'll be several regular components,' she told *Radio Times*. 'There's going to be a cooking segment, which sometimes I'll do myself, sometimes with a guest, and sometimes if I'm feeling bossy I might get someone else to do it altogether and just stand and watch. There'll be an agony component – I'm an unofficial counsellor to all of my friends. And news pieces looking at issues in terms of how they relate to people. We'll have a consumer element too – part of me is really a man ...

the part that likes boys' toys and gadgets. They'll be in. Allied to that there'll be a section looking at things in terms of value and hype. If I give people three handbags, can they tell which one cost £20 and which £450?'

She wasn't even defensive about her apparent side-stepping from prime-time Channel Four to daytime ITV, although she did tell the *Observer Food Monthly* that she considered it a 'holiday job'. 'It is always possible to merge the serious and the frivolous,' she told *Radio Times*. 'There's a certain "posh" element, as you call it, that you can enjoy unashamedly, but what you don't want to do is plunge deep into television's rivers of banality. But when you're talking to your friends you do naturally go from the banal to something that matters in your life. There's room for both, as long as you never start a conversation you're not interested in.'

As a forty-five-year-old wife and mother of two, she's confident about taking new risks. 'Without wanting to sound po-faced, if you use being known in a public sphere as a measure of success, then you're doomed to an unhappy life,' she told *Radio Times*. 'The one area in your life you can afford to have things go wrong is in work. You want to be happy at home, your family to be healthy and to have good friends. Then if you go on a stage and fall flat on your face, you can live with it.'

When she's finished the holiday job, perhaps she'll try out a books program that there was also talk of, taking her back to her first days in the literary world of Quartet and the *Sunday Times*. And maybe we will see the book that her publishers promised us back in 2001. Alison Samuel told the press that Nigella had tired – at least for the moment – of writing about recipes and was planning a book about kitchens. 'She will combine social history, design and practical tips in her next book, provisionally entitled *Kitchen*,' proclaimed the press release. Samuel, her editor at Random House, said: 'She doesn't want to write another recipe book immediately, but with this book she can still concentrate on the part of the house she loves most.'

She loves to write, and does so easily and fluidly. She explained to the Royal Society of Literature in 2004 how she put so many books together so quickly and so well. 'I think a lot and cook a lot,' she said. 'And when I finally do the writing, it all comes pouring out. Then a lot is cut. In my *Feast* book, Pumpkin Feasts was cut, as was Carb Feasts which would have been my reaction to the Atkins Diet. And then there was my Post-funeral Feast, which my publisher said would make people feel bad because of the ill-tempered foreword to that section. I said I wanted to make people feel bad. They also thought that the Texan Correction Center Last Meals would be too depressing. I said it would be interesting and fun. Why would people ask for a Diet Coke along with their burger and chips before they were going to be killed?'

'I would like to write a monograph on sandwiches in films and television. In *The West Wing*, every time somebody eats another sandwich I feel I want to write about it ... I'd love to be an academic,' she said in an interview at a civic club where she was promoting the book of *Forever Summer* through her American publisher, Hyperion. 'I wanted to stay on and do a postgraduate degree in fourteenth-century Italian lyric poetry.' 'I like a mixed portfolio,' she told Tamasin Day-Lewis after she had stopped writing her column in *The Times* to judge the Booker Prize. 'I strongly resist the notion that one can be interested in only one thing. I don't want to be put in a food ghetto.'

Her experience with *What the Papers Say*, the current affairs chat show on Radio 4 on which she and John Diamond cut their broadcasting teeth, combined with the years of filming *Nigella Bites* and *Forever Summer*, may have finally prepared her for the political chat show Janice Gabriel asked her to present all those years ago. She thinks that once the TV bug has bitten, you can never resist the pull of the lights again. 'You can never put normal people on TV,' said Janice. 'They've chosen to expose themselves, there has to be something that makes them want to put themselves through that, and they have to have that ego. She might not have had it until she saw herself on screen. When she saw that it worked, she changed.'

'She's too intelligent to become a diva,' Christopher Silvester told me. 'I think there is a tendency for people to want to believe that's what she is. She's very good about analysing her behavior and other people's behavior. She has strong convictions about how you should be towards other people.'

Her cookery programs may have inspired the way a generation eats, and boosted supermarket sales, but Janice thinks that, like Jamie Oliver, she could have done much more. 'What she could have said is, "What about all those people who cook every night? How am I going to make it easier for them to get better products in their supermarket?" She didn't use her status to do anything to change things. For a woman so bright, and who has strong political opinions, it's a shame. She's a journalist and you kind of hoped that she'd use the opportunity to write more interesting things.'

Her crew on *Nigella Bites* have been talking about another food program for the autumn of 2005, although Janice thinks that she's had her day in food TV. 'I don't think she'll come back. I think she'll write about something more serious. After the Marilyn persona, she might need to re-establish herself as a serious writer. I think she lost a lot of women by the end.'

Her famous curves have been smoothed by a personal trainer and the occasional yoga class, and the woman who never shows her legs even shocked the tabloids when she graced a London party in a badly advised flamenco outfit. As she strutted her stuff with the likes of Sir Elton John and Kevin Spacey, Nigella's figure-hugging outfit with ruffled bell-bottoms may have been in slimming black, but you can bet that Trinny and Susannah wouldn't have let her be seen in it.

I asked Sarah Johnson if she had changed much since the early days at Oxford. 'I notice that she's probably had a lot of botox recently. Her smile is different these days. I last saw her at the launch of *Feast*, and a friend said, "You've got lines, and I've got lines, but Nigella hasn't. Don't you find that odd?" She doesn't need any of that. She's very beautiful in a Marilyn Monroe sense.'

The shadow of cancer still hangs over the family, but Nigella is as sanguine as ever. 'I've learned not to dwell on the future. I suppose I do think that awful things can happen at any moment, but having children around makes you want to live in the present. You have to make things as normal as possible. I've had hugely unhappy times throughout my life,' she says, 'but I stopped being a depressive in my early thirties. These days I feel that I have a great capacity for happiness. I can take pleasure in very small things.'

Acknowledgements

Thanks to my former agent, Andrew Lownie for mentioning my name at the right time in the right place, and to my editor Sarah Hayes for allowing herself to be pestered enough to give me the job.

To Anna Arthur, Jed Novick and Bob and Nesta Smith for reading the entire draft, and for being suitably critical.

And to Jed for being a husband who can sub, edit, write, discuss, inspire, cook, clean, *and* who always thrills my soul. A real diamond geezer.

Thanks to Cuisinart for my American style food processor which helped me try out four books worth of Nigella recipes – and to LouLou and Elly for being there at my side, chopping and cutting, whisking and stirring, and being my own little domestic goddesses.

Index